The Real is not the Rational

SUNY Series in Buddhist Studies
Kenneth Inada, Editor

The
REAL
is not the
RATIONAL.

Joan Stambaugh

State University of New York Press

Preparation of this study was aided by a grant from
the National Endowment for the Humanities.

Published by
State University of New York Press, Albany

For information, address State University of New York
Press, State University Plaza, Albany, N.Y., 12246

Library of Congress Cataloging in Publication Data

Stambaugh, Joan, 1932–
    The real is not the rational.

    (SUNY series in Buddhist studies)
    Includes index.
    1. Rationalism.   2. Irrationalism (Philosophy).
3. Buddhism.   I. Title.   II. Series.
B833.S78   1986   149'.7   85–14673
ISBN 0–88706–166–4
ISBN 0–88706–167–2 (pbk.)

10   9   8   7   6   5   4   3   2   1

To Gregory

Contents

Introduction

Much of contemporary philosophy seems to be generally in a quandary with regard to the direction philosophy is to take in the future. Philosophy does not appear to be going anywhere of itself as it did, for example, for Hegel in his historical approach where one epoch followed dialectically from its predecessor in uninterrupted succession. Western philosophy seems to have exhausted its capacity to produce a new vision of reality. Nietzsche expressed this idea when he proclaimed that God is dead. The philosophical meaning of the term "God" for Nietzsche was the Platonism at the foundation of the whole Western tradition of philosophy and religion. The loss of the foundation for the highest traditional values led him to see nihilism, the "uncanny guest at the door", looming before us. Nietzsche believed that to avoid falling into the pitfall of nihilism we had to transvalue all values. This could be done successfully only by an *Übermensch*, a being who transcended anything that mankind had attained or even conceived of thus far.

Following Nietzsche's diagnosis of Western philosophy, Heidegger speaks of the end of philosophy and the task of thinking. What can the task of thinking be if we have reached the end of philosophy? And what does that mean, we have reached the end of philosophy? Heidegger's initial answer to these questions is quite clear: thinking has to move out of the domain of metaphysics. Thinking must cease to be calculative, manipulative, objectifying and learn to be attentive to what is in the world by letting it be what it is. If we allow our thinking to be changed, our way of experiencing the world and reality will also change. Much of the French tradition and some American thinkers follow him in this trend, although the individual directions diverge somewhat. Finally, Wittgenstein is one of the most radical thinkers of all in his attempt to focus philosophy in the here and now of everyday life.

Such questions go beyond the scope of this study. The study begins with two fundamental philosophical questions: what is real? and what is man? and searches back in the history of philosophy for the development of these questions. It attempts to present selected key stages in the history of the rationalist tradition, indicating the direction in which rationalism sought what is real. No attempt at value judgments is made with regard to these rationalist positions; efforts are concentrated upon understanding how the reason why for something, its cause or causes, is supposed to account for and express its reality. However, when the study considers the revolt against rationalism, some critical evaluations are necessary since it is felt that irrationalism is not a coherent, fruitful position and is certainly not the "answer" to the problems posed by rationalism. The opposite position to a point of view is always trapped in the framework of that point of view, as is clearly evidenced, for example, by Nietzsche's attempt to invert Platonism.

Thus, after examining a few key stages in the rationalist tradition, the study looks into the treatment of the *non*-rationalist tendencies within that tradition. For example, Spinoza and Leibniz discovered, almost against their intention, that there were non-rational factors that were decisive and important for human experience and even knowledge. These non-rational factors were found to be crucial to our awareness of reality, even if they never attained a central role in philosophy before the nineteenth century.

But some thinkers of the nineteenth century took these *non*-rational faculties and focussed almost exclusively on their distortion as *ir*rational ones. As often happens, the pendulum swung too far to the other side, from the rational, right past the non-rational, to the irrational.

This has been a sketchy description of the first three chapters of the study. The remaining two begin looking for alternatives to the dilemma rationalism-irrationalism. Chapter 4 turns to Heidegger who does take the non-rational (attunement, mood) seriously and who also conceives of consciousness no longer as something static possessing *faculties*, but as temporality, as process, a general direction which he shares with other thinkers and literary writers of this time. Chapter five then takes a bird's-eye look at Buddhism, an alternative tradition to our own, which obviates the dichotomy between rationalism and irrationalism because its prime concern was never with reason, but rather with the soteriological. That the treatment of an entire tradition, in many ways far more vast and complex than our own, in one chapter must perforce be at best suggestive, needs hardly be stated.

We Westerners seem to lean toward extremes, especially when confronted with something new and unfamiliar. Although pervasive exposure of the West to Eastern ideas is many decades old by now, we still tend to fall into the categories of either impatient mistrust or uncritical enthusiasm. If we can thoughtfully assimilate some elements of Eastern ideas, we can perhaps see new possibilities for philosophy, some of which are present here and there in our own tradition, but never in its mainstream. It is time, high time, for a *philosophical* encounter with the East.

This is not to say that Eastern thinking, in this study particularly Buddhism, has the "answers" to the contemporary efforts to get beyond the present situation of philosophy or to escape the confines of metaphysics. It is only hoped that Western thinkers may attempt to come thoughtfully to grips with some of the questions of the Eastern tradition, not just to breathe them in like incense. On a religious level, a good deal has been undertaken in the direction of mutual understanding. It is to be hoped now that some philosophers might try out this direction; for them, the task is more difficult. But, as Spinoza said at the conclusion of his *Ethics*: "If the way which, as I have shown, leads hither seems very difficult, it can nevertheless be found. It must indeed be difficult since it is so seldom discovered, for if salvation lay ready to hand and could be discovered without great labor, how could it be possible that it should be neglected by almost everybody? But all noble things are as difficult as they are rare."

CHAPTER 1

Reason and Causality

The questions "what is real?" and "what is man?" are two of the most fundamental problems discovered in the history of thinking. The attempts to think them out have given rise to the traditional movements in philosophy, realism and idealism, or to some other formulations of these positions. They constitute the two basic poles in the scale of possibilities for understanding the world and the *access* to that world, we ourselves. The insight that knowledge of the world or reality is inseparable from the nature of who knows it has a long history, more or less inexplicit, sometimes tending to veer so far to the one side of these two factors involved in knowledge as to deny one of them any independent existence. Locke and Berkeley, two philosophers quite close to each other in time and in many other ways as well, would be illustrations of the two extremes, Locke practically denying the mind any activity or spontaneity in Kant's sense of that term (i.e. what occurs of itself), and Berkeley stubbornly denying the existence of matter or any kind of substratum apart from our sensations.

The insight into the inseparability of knowledge of something and the nature of the knowing mind culminates with Immanuel Kant in the statement: "The conditions *a priori* of any possible experience in general are at the same time conditions of the possibility of any objects of our experience."[1] Kant is saying that the nature and constitution of the mind, i.e., the active, spontaneous, structuring categories of the understanding and passive, receptive intuitions, determine from the outset what it is *possible* for us to experience. And for Kant, the rationalist, it is possible for us to experience reality only as objects conforming to the two roots of the human understanding, sensibility and concepts.

However, the insight into the interconnectedness of man and what is called reality by no means begins with Kant, but goes back to the early Greek thinkers. Plato formulated this relation succinctly in his image of the divided line[2] where the ever ascending faculties of man (conjecture, opinion, understanding, reason) are correlated with ever ascending levels of reality (ranging from the shadow realm through the visible realm up to the Ideas themselves), progressing from the visible to the intelligible order. Plato seeks to determine what is real and how it is apprehended, and this attempt becomes decisive for centuries to follow. Of course, this relation does not subsequently remain the same or repeat itself, but undergoes radical transformations as the center of reality comes more and more to lie in the "subject," a phenomenon foreign to the Greeks in its Cartesian and post-Cartesian sense.

There is nothing earthshaking about this oversimplification of the well-known "facts" of the history of philosophy. They have been subject to a myriad of interpretations, and their presuppositions have been burrowed into. To state it briefly and by way of anticipation, our task here is to question, not to reject, the role of "reason" in man's understanding of his world and to ask how reason has *determined* his understanding of that world. We then have to examine the counter-movement to the supremacy of reason arising in the nineteenth century in its diverse forms of something akin to the "irrational". The fact that this counter-movement is thoroughly dependent upon the role of reason—in the most insidious form of dependence, reaction—should become evident in the course of discussion.

The first question to ask in the undertaking of this rather enormous task—probing the relation of reason and reality—might perhaps be: What is it that reason is supposed to accomplish and what is it looking for? The second half of that question might appear odd at first, as if reason had some kind of psychological, ulterior "motive," some particular personal "interest" in the sense in which Kant excluded interest from the aesthetic judgment,[3] searching for something special in the world.

This is not what is meant by that question. Rather, the question simply asks what kind of "answer" reason is able to give us as opposed to, for example, "answers" given by sensory experience or emotional response.

The senses give us immediate experience of the world with a minimum of "interpretation." The solipsists and others have argued that no two people have the same sense experience, for example, that no two people really see the color green in an identical way. But instead of spending a lifetime quibbling over the nuances of the color green, one can be satisfied for practical purposes that there is sufficient agreement among most people to function with a fairly common idea of what green is. Far more important factors come into play when a real involvement is at stake, which can hardly be the case with bare sense experience, which is a matter of artificial abstraction anyhow. I am "involved" with experiences when it concerns me at a deeper existential, intellectual or emotional level than that of sheerly staring at something. The artificial paradigm of Cartesian clear and distinct ideas is based on this kind of staring observation and completely stifles the question of any kind of concern with an object or response to it. This may sound at first like the worst kind of subjectivism, but it is not. There are so many unquestioned and unasked difficulties with the staunch accusation of subjectivism that it is best to leave it aside for now. To raise this accusation one would first of all have to know what one really meant by the term "subjective," a term which immediately puts everyone who uses it—and who does not?—on the court bench of judgment levying with aplomb the "objective" accusation of merely personal opinion.

We leave this topic for now and return to our question, what does reason look for? Reason looks for a reason why. To have knowledge of something does not just mean to have experience of it—this is too "vague"—but is rather equivalent to finding out why it is, its "cause." For instance, if I witness a family argument, it is not sufficient to have sense experience of the conversation, to hear the voices and see the gestures or gesticulations, it is not even enough to be familiar with the members of that family. I have to know most of the factors involved leading up to the argument; I have to know how and why that argument came about. And most of these factors lie in the *past*. The present situation is simply the unravelling result of past factors. Or if I see a bank robbery, again mere sense observation will not tell me enough of what is going on to understand the situation. To fully comprehend it, I would have to know how the robbery was planned, who was involved in carrying it out (perhaps waiting outside), what the loot was, and so forth. Or, finally, if I feel ill, my state of queasiness or pain is an unpleasant sensation which may give me little or no knowledge at all of what is the matter with me, but precisely force me to find out what the matter is (or go to a doctor), and to find the reason for my illness and then hopefully, of course, the cure. A pragmatic doctor may have learned to be content with a cure that works; the patient almost invariably wants to know what the cause was, why this happened to him. Only then does he "know" what is the matter with him.

In the *Theatetus*, a dialogue which makes libraries of contemporary "epistemology" superfluous, Socrates struggles to inquire into the nature of knowledge. After testing the possible answers that knowledge is perception or that knowledge is true belief, he comes up with the third possibility that knowledge is true belief with the addition of an "account" (*logos*). He then pursues three meanings of account: expressing ourselves in speech (*legein*), enumerating the elements of a thing and, finally, being able to name some mark by which the thing in question differs from everything else.[4] Even though Socrates rejects the final definition of knowledge as true belief plus an account in the third sense named above as designating the distinguishing mark of something, even though he rejects it as being worse than the most vicious of circles since true belief would already have to include knowledge of the distinguishing mark of something, this last definition comes as close to telling us what knowledge is as any other possibility discussed in the dialogue. As often the case in Plato's dialogues, particularly the earlier ones, the reader does not get an "answer"—even the "proofs" for the immortality of the soul, for example, in the *Phaedo* don't give any "answers"— but he finds out and knows a great deal more about the subject than before. Thus the final definition is not a complete flop, an "unreal phantom" unmasked by the philosophical midwife Socrates, but tells us, as does the whole dialogue, something about the nature of knowledge. In any case, it is far better to inquire in this manner than to be one "whose mind has never conceived at all."

Of course, for Plato knowledge of a thing is ultimately knowledge of the Idea or Form of a thing. I only know what justice is when my reason attains knowledge of absolute Justice. Any particular instantiation of justice will never tell me what it is "in and by itself in its own place."

Plato's doctrine of Ideas or Forms is too vast and complicated a subject to go into here in any depth. Pursuing our question of reason's search for a reason why, reason in this case sends us straight to the Platonic Idea. The Idea is the reason why or cause for something in the very non-descriptive, non-informative sense that things are what they are by virtue of their imitation of or participation in the Idea. To say that this kind of explanation is non-descriptive and non-informative simply means that Plato in giving the Idea as cause accounts for the *essence* of a thing; he does not really account for the actual factual *existence* of a particular thing nor for its shortcomings in failing to measure up to the Idea. Plato is not interested in a thing's actual existence since that belongs to the realm of becoming and change. It is the object of opinion and conjecture, not reason, and is precisely what Plato wants to get beyond. Thus the essence (Idea) of a thing is its ultimate reason why and the kind of causal explanation involved indicates the relationship of the thing to its Idea, a relationship of imitation or participation.

Imitation and participation are surely not mutually exclusive and are probably closer to each other than they seem on first reading. What imitates something in a sense also participates in it and what participates in something also imitates it. If, for example, a student imitates or emulates a teacher, he also participates in the reality of that teacher—in what he is, does and knows. And if someone participates, say, in a group demonstration, he is to an extent "imitating" in his actions what the others do.

There is a kind of "teleology" in Plato's treatment of causality; a striving (*eros*) which always refers the ultimate cause to the Idea. Plato (and Aristotle) continually rebuke Anaxagoras for having discovered the principle of *nous* (mind) and then failing to use it to explain anything. Rather, Plato feels, Anaxagoras falls back into mechanistic descriptions when he wants to explain why. Finally, in the *Phaedo*, when Socrates puts the question *why* he is sitting in prison, he marvels that anyone would want to give his bones and sinews as that reason. Of course he cannot *sit* (or stand or lie) without bones and sinews, but they explain nothing, they are merely the *condition* of his sitting. The real reason is mind, Socrates' striving for knowledge of the Absolute. Expressed in contemporary terminology, it is very difficult, almost ridiculous to try to explain human intentionality in terms of mechanistic and materialistic causes. A student is not in a classroom because he has walked up a flight of stairs, gone thirty feet down the corridor, and turned left into a room and sat down on a chair. He is presumably there because he wants to learn something.

In seeking the reason why in an eternal *eidos* (essence, Idea), reason *abandons* the actual present reality of what is in question. In *explaining* something, one goes back or "up" (our language is inundated with these "spatial" expressions) to something *else* which is *responsible* for the present reality. This statement is not meant to be restricted to Plato, but by way of anticipation it more or less applies to all causal explanations, to the whole attitude and intent behind asking the question why.

Aristotle stated at the beginning of his *Metaphysics* that all men by nature desire to know. This is true of man in contrast to the other animals who have only sensation and sometimes memory, but not reason which makes man capable of molding his experience into art and science. In the *Politics*[5] Aristotle states that animals mostly lead a life of nature and sometimes are influenced by habit, but that man in addition to nature and habit has rational principle. He then proceeds to divide the soul of man into two parts, one having a rational principle in itself and the other lacking such a principle but capable of obeying it. We shall leave the question of "soul" aside for now, reserving it for a discussion of the role assigned to the "*faculties*" of man other than reason.[6]

The context of Aristotle's discussion of man's faculties is

education, and he is attempting to find out which faculties it is conducive to educate and how. In contrast to some of our modern methods of education, Aristotle's method does not take a finished quantity of information and advise that it be presented to or forced upon the learner, for example, in the way in which a computer is programmed. Our whole educational jargon is tainted with computer language, though we are often no longer even aware of it. We speak of input and output, feedback etc. as though all the teacher has to do is to program the student with some information and out it comes at the right time (*kairos*), i.e. the exam, only to be subsequently lost and forgotten just as the computer presumably "forgets" its old programs no longer in operation. No, Aristotle is not concerned with the body of material to be transmitted, but with its effect on the learner and his faculties. His question is how will this or that subject shape and strengthen and harmonize the learner. In this connection I cannot resist citing a passage from the *Politics*:

> Besides, children should have something to do, and the rattle of Archytas, which people give to their children in order to amuse them and prevent them from breaking anything in the house, was a capital invention, for a young thing cannot be quiet. The rattle is a toy suited to the infant mind, and education is a rattle or toy for children of a larger growth.[7]

Children have to have something to do, presumably not only children, and this something to do might just as well lead somewhere, namely, for Aristotle, to the furtherance of rational principle and mind which are the end toward which nature strives.[8] We are not born endowed with a rational way of life; it is a state to be sought after and developed.

In these passages cited, and in others not cited, lie the seeds of the understanding of man, prefigured and more or less paralleled in Plato, of man as the living being which has "reason" (*zoon logon echon*). This understanding gets crystallized into the latinized version of Aristotle and yields the traditional definition of man as the *animal rationale*, the rational animal. The problem that *logos* and *ratio* by no means coincide is important, but need not concern us here.

The definition of man as the rational animal, the animal which has reason, became decisive for all subsequent understanding of man, including the multifarious revolts against reason, whether in the form of the irrational, the unconscious, Marxism, the existential, or the absurd. This is a sweeping statement, but not a particularly new or unfamiliar one, and, moreover, a pretty undeniable one. One is, of course, immediately prompted to ask: well, besides the rational and/or the irrational, what else is there? This question is difficult to answer precisely because "whatever else there is" has been stuffed into the category of the irrational due to the entrenchment and supremacy of reason. Whatever is not rational is irrational, whether it be condemned or extolled as such. What the later chapters of this study will attempt to do is to discuss faculties of man other than reason which do not exclude reason and are not "irrational."

To return to the Greeks and our central topic of the interconnectedness of reason and causality, let us examine how first Plato and then Aristotle with their trust in the supremacy of reason treated the other faculties of man such as emotion, desire, appetite, pleasure and pain and so on. Because of the richness of his thought, it is impossible to pin Plato down to any one-sided, pat view of man's faculties apart from that of reason. However, he has much to say about them which yields a coherent direction, especially when he is talking about the soul.

By way of preface, one might try to ask the somewhat amorphous question why Plato or, for that matter, anyone, places the non-rational faculties so low on the ontological ladder. Some of the answers to this question are obvious, but their further implications and the grounds leading up to them are less so. The senses which give us our visual, auditory etc. experience and the senses in the broader meaning of that word which give us feelings of pleasure and pain, as well as the various emotions, are all radically subject to change and becoming. It is this incontrovertible fact that leads Plato for the most part to condemn the body, not some pseudo-religious horror of "body" as such. *There is no constancy possible* for the body. Its experiences (sensations) are immediate, never distanced by the mediation of reason. The senses have no choice, they are instantaneously passive to what affects them. If I place my hand on a hot radiator, no mediation in the world can distance that immediate sensation of heat for me. According to Plato, all of the non-rational faculties are immersed in this realm of constant change and becoming. They can never attain the good itself, virtue itself, justice itself, the Forms forever inacessible to the senses and feelings, forever untouched by anything tainted by the realm of becoming. "Reality" cannot be something which we can *lose*, it cannot be something which "goes away," therefore it can never be found in the realm of body and becoming.

To indicate just a few of Plato's discussions of soul and body, I should like to mention a passage in the *Phaedo*, and the two images for the soul in the *Republic* and the *Phaedrus*. The *Phaedo* is admittedly one of the most "dualistic" of Plato's dialogues, but there is much in it which never gets significantly modified in the later works, for instance, the image or idea that the soul "sinks" down to the body, takes roots and grows there.

Before philosophy takes it over, says Socrates, the soul is a helpless prisoner chained in the body viewing reality only through its prison bars and wallowing in ignorance. The body is indeed the prison of the soul. Why is the soul imprisoned in this way? Socrates tells us that the imprisonment is "effected by the prisoner's own active desire"; he is first accessory to his own confinement. Here, as in the myth of Er in the *Republic* ("The blame is his who chooses, God is blameless,") it is always the individual's own responsibility and choice which answer for his situation, never the gods or some kind of inexorable, external fate. The task of the soul is to realize the deceptiveness of the senses, try to abstain from all desires, pleasures and griefs and to concentrate itself by itself. The greatest danger in becoming addicted to desires and pleasures, Socrates points out, is something the sufferer does not even recognize. The danger inherent in the senses and their orientation toward visible things in the realm of becoming is that these kinds of things cause the most violent emotion, and this the soul takes to be what is most real. Socrates is saying precisely that what is most immediate, direct and "intense" is not what is most real, but is rather what rivets the soul to the body, imprisoning it more and more deeply and preventing any possibility of its escape.

In the *Phaedrus* Socrates states that there are two sorts of ruling or guiding principles within all of us, an innate desire for pleasure and an acquired judgment that aims at what is best. The first principle, if not constantly restrained by the second, is irrational,[10] and pursues the enjoyment of beauty. Socrates then talks about the immortality of the soul. It is a first principle, it neither comes into being nor does it perish, and its nature is self-motion. A body deriving its motion from a source within itself is besouled (animated). Socrates then goes on to try to describe the nature of the soul above and beyond its quality of self-motion which vouches for its immortality. He is well aware of the difficulty of his task.

> As to the soul's immortality we have said enough, but as to its nature there is this that must be said. What manner of thing it is would be a long tale to tell, and most assuredly a god alone could tell it, but what it resembles, that a man might tell in briefer compass.[11]

Like the image in the *Republic*, the image for the soul in the *Phaedrus* is tripartite, comprising a charioteer, a noble and good steed, and a steed with the opposite character. In the case of the gods, the winged steeds and their winged charioteers are all good, and form an indissoluble union of powers. In the case of man, it is ultimately the task and responsibility of the charioteer to subdue the wicked steed and keep it from corrupting the good steed. The "union of powers" is not native and indissoluble, but acquired and constantly maintained only with great effort and toil. The charioteer is likened to reason, the soul's pilot[11] which alone can behold true being and have veritable knowledge of being that veritably is.[12]

Finally, the image of the soul at the end of book IX of the *Republic*[13] is set in the context of a discussion of justice and injustice. Socrates wants to show that any sort of injustice will throw the soul completely off balance by nourishing its lower parts and stifling and enfeebling the rational human element. The three parts of the soul in this image are a beast with many heads continually springing forth, molded into a single shape, a lion and, smallest of all, a man. They are joined in one so as in some sort to grow together, and the resultant likeness is that of a man. In other words, to the observer the likeness appears to be one living creature, man, whereas if one could look within, the man would be the smallest part of all, quite tiny in comparison with the other clamorous parts, the most delicate part, overshadowed by the lion and above all by the many-headed beast. Socrates' main concern is that any kind of injustice in the sense of nurturing the lower parts of the soul at the expense of the higher will "emancipate that dread, that huge and manifold beast overmuch."[14]

Without being identical, the two images for the soul are very close in their tripartite structure and in the description of the various parts. The soul consists basically of irrational desire and reason with a relatively "neutral" component in between which is capable of being influenced in either direction. The task of the soul is to free itself as far as possible in this life from the irrational, from the body, the senses, pleasure and pain, and ascend beyond the realm of the visible to true being.

What is important in this delineation of well-known elements of Plato's thought is the absolute emphasis on reason alone, either as maintaining justice in the soul or state or else in its higher flights to the upper region. Reason seeks for the eternal, the changeless, the Form or Idea of justice, beauty, temperance, ultimately of the Good. These Ideas are the causes of the imperfect likenesses which we know. They furnish a reason why anything is at all, although they are not responsible for the imperfection which invariably and inevitably creeps into the likenesses. Reason, the highest part of the soul, strives to know the ultimate reason why.

The remainder of this chapter will be concerned with the further development of causality and the reason why after Plato. After this brief review of the direction which the supremacy of reason took, we shall try to examine the role of the non-rational faculties within the rationalist tradition (Chapter 2). It might be that we have no adequate *names* for those possibilities which Plato, for instance, divorced from reason and shunted off to the domain of the irrational. If the response to a painting is somehow "pleasurable" (this is, of course, a whole complicated subject in itself), is it for that reason *eo ipso* "irrational"?

Aristotle expresses dissatisfaction with Plato's treatment of causality, and proceeds to give a far more differentiated discussion of it. Whereas the framework of Plato's remarks on cause is generally the relation of the particular to the universal (the relation of this just man to justice itself), Aristotle rejects this relation as a causally operative one. Aristotle's interest in the particular leads him to analyze all of the factors involved in physical change and to come up with a plurality of "causes" in a broad sense of that word. There are ten factors invovled in his analysis: the specific and the general, potentiality and actuality, the four causes proper, chance and spontaneity. In contradistinction to Plato, generic effects for Aristotle are to be assigned to generic causes, particular effects to particular causes. Statues in general are produced by sculptors in general, this particular statue was produced by this particular sculptor. There is no direct interaction between the universal and the particular. Then, the potential cause of a house is a house-builder, the actual cause is a house-builder-building. With his concepts of potentiality and actuality, Aristotle can explain the nature of change and bridge the either/or dichotomy of is/is-not, of a thing's existence or non-existence. A house-builder does not cease to be a house-builder when not engaged in building; he merely ceases to be an actual house-builder-building and becomes a potential one.

Aristotle's doctrine of the four causes takes into account the—in his opinion—partial theories of causality of his predecessors, both those of the early physicists and Plato. His doctrine is inclusive enough to incorporate what Plato had called a condition (i.e. the material cause of Socrates' sitting, his bones and sinews) and also to account for such factors as chance and spontaneity. Thus Aristotle enumerates the material, formal, efficient[15] and final causes, often using the example of a statue. In the example of the statue, the bronze is its material cause, that out of which it is made; the formal cause is the idea of, say, Apollo which the sculptor has in mind; the efficient cause is the sculptor himself and the final cause is the finished statue which the sculptor wishes to attain.

Finally, chance and spontaneity complete Aristotle's list of the ten factors involved in causality. They differ in that chance is a factor in the sphere of moral (human) action, whereas spontaneity is a wider, less determinate term applicable to the lower animals and inanimate objects. "Spontaneous" means "of itself." The stone which falls and hits a man had and could have had no intention of doing so, and the horse who suddenly moves in a certain direction presumably could not have intended to do so either. To update Aristotle's example for chance, I might go to a football game and run into someone who owes me ten dollars and who, upon meeting me, actually pays it back. I did not go to the football game for the purpose of retrieving my money; it happened "by chance."

This summary of Aristotle's analysis of causality should serve to outline the possible meanings of the reason why, some present in his predecessors, some to be developed on a quite different ontological foundation by later thinkers. Nothing is principally inexplicable for Aristotle. It may not be able to be anticipated or predicted, but it can be understood and explained. Even chance is "rational."

A detailed discussion of the later history of causality is not possible here. Keeping in mind our question of the nature of reality, it will be sufficient for our purposes to single out a few significant shifts in the development of causality in the attempt to see what happens in the interpretation and explanation of reality.

First of all, there are two fundamental points to bear in mind during the remainder of this discussion of causality. On the one hand, the components of Aristotle's analysis are reduced to two basic kinds of cause, the efficient and the final, and these two remain the principal ways of explaining the world process down to the time of contemporary physics. The fact that the question of causality is focussed on the world process already contains implicitly the second point. The question of causality is brought to bear, not on this or that thing or process, but more and more on a greater and greater totality. In keeping with the increasing attempt in modern philosophy to "systematize" knowledge, the inquiry with regard to causality shifts from the nature of particular processes to the interconnectedness and unity of the whole in a way surely implicit in the earlier thinkers but by no means carried out to such a conscious degree that strives for certainty and, finally, for "absoluteness." The final step in this shift is from the causality of the world process to that of the first cause and originator of that process, to God. Thus causality comes to play its principal role in the "proofs" of God's existence, efficient causality answering the question of the origin of the world, how it started (cosmological proof), and final causality answering the question of the design and purpose of the world (teleological proof).

Whatever the intricacies of these proofs may mean, they serve to finalize the position of supremacy for causality in all philosophical questioning. A brief look at four thinkers, Descartes, Leibniz, Kant and Hegel might serve to conclude these remarks on causality for the time being.

In his third *Meditation* Descartes brings a proof for the existence of God which involves the somewhat complex and very controversial *relation* of an idea in the intellect to its "cause" by something existing in reality. The fundamental principle which Descartes appeals to again and again is that there must be at least as much reality in the efficient and total cause as in its effect. "For, pray, whence can the effect derive its reality if not from its cause?" Two corollaries are implicitly contained here, that something cannot come from nothing, and what is more perfect cannot proceed from what is less perfect. Hence the idea of a perfect being, an idea of infinite substance which has more "objective[16] reality must have as its cause such a perfect being which actually[17] exists. In his argument Descartes summarizes most of the possible objections to this proof without really getting around or much beyond its basic flaws and difficulties. The idea of a perfect, infinite being cannot be sheerly negative, i.e. it cannot be the mere logical negation of Descartes' own finitude. On the contrary, Descartes can say that he would not even know that he was finite if he did not previously have the notion of what is infinite. How could he know what is imperfect if he did not already have the standard of perfection, an infinite being, by which to judge his own imperfection? Nor can he arrive at the idea of a perfect being by increasing the degrees of perfection of his knowledge into infinity since this procedure is precisely a mark of his finitude. He can never in this way arrive at a knowledge of God since this increase of knowledge is shot through and through with potentiality. It never arrives at a point where it could no longer increase, and thus cannot bridge the gap between potential, increasing knowledge and actual knowledge of an actually infinite God. Thirdly, the idea of an infinite perfect being cannot be produced by several causes scattered throughout the universe. Since unity is one of the principal perfections of God, the idea must be produced by one actually existing being. Finally, Descartes concludes that he who has this idea could not even *exist* if no such perfect being exists (and there goes the *fundamentum inconcussum* of the *cogito*). For while his parents may be the cause of his biological being, they are not the cause of him as a thinking thing nor are they anything more than the initial cause of even his biological being. Whoever considers the nature of time will realize that it by no means follows from the fact that he existed in the past that he will continue to exist in the future unless some cause produces him anew at every instant (*creatio continua*). And since he is not conscious of any such power within himself to conserve his own being, he is radically dependent on another, perfect being to preserve him.

It is Leibniz who elevates the principle of causality to the status of a fundamental principle not only on equal footing with but ultimately surpassing the principles of identity and contradiction. All of our thinking, according to Leibniz, is based upon two great principles, the principle of contradiction which is the principle of possibility, and the principle of sufficient reason which is the principle of reality. These two principles are aligned with the two kinds of truth, truths of reasoning and truths of fact. Truths of reasoning based on the principle of contradiction are necessary and their opposite is impossible. They are valid as logical, geometrical and arithmetical laws. Truths of fact based upon the principle of sufficient reason are contingent and their opposite is possible. These truths concern the entire world of experience, the world of physics, which Leibniz ultimately hopes to ground in metaphysics. Since truths of fact contain no *internal* reason why something is so and not otherwise (their opposite is possible), their reason why must lie outside of them. Since Leibniz is not content with mechanism as the sole causal explanation of the world, he consciously returns to what he calls the substantial forms of the schoolmen, not to explain the details of physics or particular phenomena (this would be inadmissible), but in order to understand the ultimate principles of the universe and, most of all, the realms of mind and incorporeal nature. In other words, Leibniz brings back final causes in addition to mechanical causation, thus positing two different kinds of causality applicable to two different realms.

> Souls act according to the laws of final causes, by appetitions, ends and means. Bodies act in accordance with the laws of efficient causes or of motion. And the two realms, that of efficient causes and that of final causes, are in harmony with each other."[18]

On the surface of it, Leibniz appears to be content with mechanistic causation as an explanation for the physical world, the realm of nature, as were most of his recent predecessors and contemporaries. His innovation lies in returning to final causes, the "substantial forms," for intelligent action, for souls and the realm of grace.

> As we have above established a perfect harmony between two natural kingdoms, the one of efficient, the other of final causes, we should also notice here another harmony between the physical kingdom of nature and the moral kingdom of grace; that is, between God considered as the architect of the mechanism of the universe and God considered as monarch of the divine city of spirits.[19]

Thus Leibniz bifurcates causality into two realms, that of the mechanism of the world and that of the teleology of spirits. Underlying this distinction is the distinction of the physical and the metaphysical so that it is ultimately not so much a matter of two independent realms, but rather of one realm, the physical, *grounded* in the other, the metaphysical. The restricting phrase "not so much" is necessary here because Leibniz never quite succeeds in banishing a certain hesitation to relinquish the independence of mechanical causation. In general, he shows a certain ambivalence with regard to the two kinds of causation, an ambivalence which he finally resolves through his principle of preestablished harmony. On the one hand, he shares with

Plato and Aristotle the dissatisfaction with mere mechanical or efficient causation since it is incapable of explaining purposive action or even perception.

> It must be confessed, moreover, that *perception* and that which depends on it are *inexplicable by mechanical causes*, that is by figures and motions. And, supposing that there were a machine so constructed as to think, feel and have perception, we could conceive of it as enlarged and yet preserving the same proportions, so that we might enter it as into a mill. And this granted, we should only find on visiting it, pieces which push one against another, but never anything by which to explain a perception.[20]

And in the *Discourse on Metaphysics*, which repeatedly takes up this problem, he cites "those ancients who regarded the physicists as impious when they maintained that not Jupiter thundered but some material which is found in the clouds." On the other hand, Leibniz is curiously reluctant to relegate efficient causality to a secondary position, perhaps because he is keenly aware of the dangers of the Scholasticism he had readopted in the substantial forms. In one passage, final causality even sounds like a mere pragmatic makeshift.

> "Yet I find that the method of efficient causes, which goes much deeper and is in a measure more immediate and *a priori* [!], is also more difficult when we come to details, and I think that our philosophers are still very frequently far removed from making the most of this method. The method of final causes, however, is easier and can be frequently employed to find out important and useful truths which we should have to seek for a long time if we were confined to that other more physical method..."[21]

Leibniz concludes that "the best plan would be to join the two ways of thinking."[22] In the last analysis, however, final causes win the battle, and when the principle of sufficient reason enters the fray, it is very much the garb of final causality and intelligent choice that it wears, particularly when the question of God and the creation of the world are at stake.

It appears more and more clear that although all the particular phenomena of nature can be explained mathematically by those who understand them, yet nevertheless, the general principles of corporeal nature and even of mechanics are metaphysical rather than geometric, and belong rather to certain indivisible forms or natures as the causes of the appearances, than to the corporeal mass or to extension.[23]

The principle of sufficient reason is for Leibniz *the* "grand principle" of everything, so to speak, the fulcrum of the world and the relation of God to the world as well. One would almost have to say that Leibniz was obsessed with his grand principle which, after all, he neither invented nor discovered. He is aware that it is not a completely innovative principle, but he feels that although previous thinkers were familiar with it, they did not make sufficient use of it nor appreciate its meaning fully. A full understanding of it would dispense with all of the falsities and misconceptions which Leibniz was combatting, i.e., the void, atoms, Newton's absolute space and time as the "sensorium" of God, the question of "miracles," fatalism, chance. The list is endless, and everything is pretty much interconnected.

In the remainder of this discussion of Leibniz we shall examine the principle of sufficient reason and its relation to the two principles of contradiction and of identity (which Leibniz thinks anew), and to "preestablished harmony." The full formulation reads as follows:

Thus far we have spoken as simple *physicists*: now we must advance to *metaphysics*, making use of the *great principle*, little employed in general, which teaches that *nothing happens without a sufficient reason*; that is to say, nothing happens without its being possible for him who should sufficiently understand things, to give a reason sufficient to determine why it is so and not otherwise. This principle laid down, the first question which should rightly be asked, will be, *Why is there something rather than nothing?* For nothing is simpler and easier than something. Further, suppose that things must exist, we must be able to give a reason *why they must exist so* and not otherwise.[24]

The new emphasis which Leibniz brings to bear on the question of causality lies in his understanding of the word *suf-*

ficient. Not only must everything have a cause (the old principle that something cannot come from nothing—*ex nihilo nihil fit*). It must also and above all have a cause why it is *just as it is* and *not otherwise*. Here Leibniz is walking the tight rope between necessity (fatalism) and chance (arbitrariness, not freedom in any fruitful sense). And this principle must apply to everything within the world and, above all, to the fact that there *is* a world, to the fact that there *is* something rather than nothing. The world does not simply follow of necessity from the nature of God as Spinoza would have it. This would amount to fatalism and destroy freedom in God. Rather, the world must be *chosen* by God according to the principle of fitness and what is best. The world does not follow from God; he does not have to create it. He chooses to do so. Why? Because not to create the world would have entailed less perfection, and this is contrary to the nature of God who always chooses what is best. The synthesis of variety and order in the world make it more perfect than if no world existed, and more perfect than any other possible world.

"Why is there something rather than nothing? For nothing is simpler and easier than something." But given Leibniz' conception of the highest being, the *ultima ratio*, there is no reason why he would want this kind of simplicity which is merely simpler than something. The kind of simplicity appropriate to God is that of the *unity* of the manifold, the highest possible synthesis of variety and order. The concept of synthesis becomes crucial here. It will later dominate the thinking of Kant, and in a different way that of Hegel.

In the various traditional versions of the ontological argument for God's existence, perfection always includes existence, beginning with Anselm's whose formulation of it had the most original power. That than which nothing greater can be thought is more adequate to the concept of God than the highest being of Descartes because it means, strictly speaking, that God cannot be an object of finite thinking; he transcends it by definition, whereas the highest being is, at least in principle, an object of thought. For Leibniz, the best of all possible worlds entails the fact that not only does God's absolute perfection necessarily involve his existence, but the very nature and *essence* of the finite creature strives for as much perfection as possible, i.e., for existence.

> From the very fact that something exists rather than nothing, there is in possible things, that is, in the very possibility or essence, a certain exigent need of existence, and, so to speak, some claim to existence; in a word that *essence tends of itself toward existence* (italics mine)[25]

Further:

> And as possibility is the principle of essence, so perfection or the degree of essence . . . is the principle of existence.

What is perfection? Perfection is the quantity of essence. Essence tends of itself toward existence. Leibniz is not only saying, as did his predecessors, that God's perfection must include existence, otherwise there would be another being still more perfect because he possessed still another quality, i.e. existence. He is saying that perfection as quantity of essence *tends of itself* toward existence, and this is true not only of God, but insofar as possible it is true of all finite beings.[22] For finite beings, essence does not necessarily *entail* existence, as it does for God. They—in Leibniz' unusual expression—*incline* toward existence. To speak metaphorically, they would *rather* exist than not.

Leibniz extricates himself from the Scylla and Charibdis of necessity and contingency or chance by positing what he calls *hypothetical* or *consequential* necessity. It applies to God's choice to create the world, and to voluntary actions in general. Once the choice is made, there is a kind of internal necessity which follows that choice which was, nevertheless, free because its opposite or another alternative would also have been possible. Leibniz places metaphysical, absolute, mathematical necessity, *essence*, on the one side and moral necessity, inclining without necessitating, *existence*, on the other. Again we have the realm of nature and the realm of grace, mechanical causation and teleological causation, ruled by different principles. Leibniz explains the freedom of God in creating the world by saying that

He has the *power* to create any sort of world, but His *wisdom* and *goodness* lead Him, according to the principle of fitness, to choose the best, this world and no other. With the idea of choice according to the principle of fitness, Leibniz emphatically rejects Spinoza for whom the world *follows from* God. The world has a sufficient reason why it must be just so and not otherwise, i.e. God, "the ultimate reason of things."

In order not to get lost in the intriguing intricacies of Leibniz' arguments for the creation of the world, let us finally review his basic principles of sufficient reason, the identity of indiscernibles and preestablished harmony, and then proceed to Kant's view of causality.

> Those great principles of *sufficient reason* and of the *identity of indiscernibles*, change the state of metaphysics.[28]

The principle of sufficient reason leads Leibniz to formulate his own version of the principle of identity, the identity of indiscernibles. The principle of sufficient reason always gives a reason, not to act in general, but to act in a certain particular manner.

> For a man never has a sufficient reason to *act*, when he has not also a sufficient reason to act *in a certain particular manner*.[29]

The qualification "sufficient" requires a "so and not otherwise" which absolutely precludes the possibility of two exactly identical things in the world. Two identical things in the world are impossible and unthinkable on at least two grounds, logical and theological. Logically, if, to take Leibniz' example, two leaves were exactly identical in every way, i.e. color, shape, texture, markings etc., if they did not differ, at least, in spatial position, be that difference ever so minute, they would have to be the same leaf. On theological grounds, the possibility of two identical things in the world would undermine the principle of *sufficient* reason in God and subject Him to a chaotic arbitrariness.

> I infer from that principle, among other consequences, that there are not in nature *two* real, absolute beings, *indiscernible*

from each other; because if there were, God and nature would act without reason, in ordering the one otherwise than the other.[30]

Thus the *sufficiency* of sufficient reason requires that, once a choice has been made, this and no other thing is the result. Choice is not choice in general and *überhaupt*, but choice of one particular thing. Sufficient reason is not a reason why in general, but a reason why just so and not otherwise.

Finally, some mention should at least be made of Leibniz' principle of preestablished harmony, by which he synchronizes the two orders of mechanism (body) and teleology (soul) and by which he can also explain the theory that the "windowless" monads, who have no possible direct contact with each other "from the outside," nevertheless experience the same world in differing degrees of clarity. Preestablished harmony is God's *fiat* at the creation of the world. God is compared to a watchmaker who adjusts the mechanical realm of body and matter to the teleological realm of soul, once and for all at the creation of things. When Clarke objects that this requires a perpetual miracle, Leibniz replies that it is one, original miracle, though indeed "it is a perpetual *wonder*, as many natural things are."[31] And when Clarke objects that the term preestablished harmony is a "term of art," Leibniz agrees, but states that it "is not a term that explains nothing."[32]

We shall interrupt this discussion for now, but return to Leibniz in the next chapter on the non-rational faculties which he in particular thinks in an innovative way. To summarize briefly, Leibniz' almost obsessive fascination with the principle of sufficient reason, with the *principe grande*, leads him to place this formulation of causality at the very foundation of his thought. Correctly understood, the principle of sufficient reason guarantees the principle of identity, the identity of indiscernibles, since it explains why a thing must be just *so* and not otherwise, thus identical with itself and with no other. The principle of sufficient reason ultimately requires preestablished harmony. Sufficient reason is the most basic form of causality, based on the principle of fitness and perfection. Since Leibniz is not quite willing to ground the other kind of causality, mechanism, in sufficient reason, preestablished harmony accounts for the co-ordination and agreement of the two kinds of causality, of the realms of nature and grace. And finally, the principle of sufficient reason as the principle of existence itself is intimately bound up with Leibniz' concept of substance as *vis*, force. The very essence of things is to strive for existence. In all possible things, i.e., in the very essence of things, there is a "certain exigent need of existence." Perfection or the degree of essence possible for a finite being limited by receptivity and perspective, is the principle of existence. The most extreme instance of this characteristic of essence tending to exist is God who alone exists of absolute necessity and is supramundane, transcendent to the world.

It is Kant who transposes the problem of causality to human consciousness, thus shifting the emphasis from that of causality as a reason why to that of the question of the conditions for the possibility of knowledge. Causality becomes what makes possible, and to inquire into causality is to inquire into the structure of the human mind, how it is able to know. By "conditions" (of possibility) Kant does not simply mean a necessary auxillary factor, as Plato did in the case of Socrates' bones and sinews being the condition, but not the real cause, of his sitting in prison. Rather, the conditions of the possibility of knowledge constitute the universal structure of the finite human mind. They are universal, common to all, and subjective, i.e. they refer to the finite human mind perceiving phenomena, and not to objects in themselves, things as they are without relation to a knowing subject. This "transcendental turn" of Kant's shifts all inquiry from the focus on objects to the focus on the condition of the possibility of knowledge of those objects. "I entitle *transcendental* all knowledge which is occupied not so much with objects as with the mode of our knowledge of objects insofar as this mode of knowledge is to be possible *a priori*."[33]

The problem of causality in Kant's thinking is complex, but not really complicated if we restrict it to the purposes of our inquiry. Like the question of the self which appears on different levels of Kant's analysis (form of inner intuition, transcendental apperception and the Idea of the soul), causality is also a constituent factor for different levels of experience and thinking. And like the question of the self, causality straddles the division of phenomena and noumena, of appearances and things in themselves. But the question of causality is able to become constitutive and meaningful in the noumenal realm in a way that the question of the self cannot. By way of anticipation it can be said that Leibniz' bifurcation of causality into the mechanism of the realm of nature and the teleology of the realm of grace, a problem which he solved by recourse to preestablished harmony set up between the two by God, becomes the division of the strictly ordered causality of phenomena and the implicitly noumenal causality through freedom in human action and morality. However, the transformation of the problem is not quite this *pat*, and we must focus on the problem as it is a question for Kant in the framework of his "critical" thinking. What is supremely important for Kant is precisely the question of causality through freedom, the question of man not merely as a creature of nature, bound absolutely to knowing only phenomena but never able to know the noumenal realm of things in themselves (the cosmos, the soul and God, or more specifically and "existentially," crucial to human interest, the immortality of the soul and the existence of God), but man as a free being in his moral actions. The question of *freedom* was implicit but not problematic in pre-critical philosophy. Since Kant rules out the *knowledge* of a supreme Being for finite human cognition and since we thus cannot know that we are created free by this Being, human freedom becomes the crux of his whole philosophical enterprise. It is the avenue of escape from the austere framework of limiting conditions which he placed upon our knowledge. It is the sole chance of getting from the realm of phenomena to that of noumena in a valid way because human freedom is a *fact of experience*. Instead of the understanding and reason spinning transcendent (having no possible relation to experience) cobwebs by itself, we can start from the fact that human beings are at least capable of being free, and this fact, being rooted in the realm of experience, includes the factor of sensuous intuition so crucially important to Kant. The fact of freedom shows us that we are not completely determined by what precedes and conditions us, as are other beings of nature, but we are capable of initiating action. We are capable of acting in accordance with final purposes, and final purposes are purposes which need no other as condition of their possibility.[34]

The importance and far-reaching scope of the question of causality for Kant is evident in some of the more difficult and technical passages of the *Critique of Pure Reason* which we shall merely point out here briefly. It is not really necessary to go into these passages in detail since that would constitute another study in its own right. Our problem is more simple. We are only attempting to follow what happens to the two kinds of causality in Kant and to see where they lead.

But the intimate connection between causality and the real for Kant should at least be pointed out. In tracing some of the history of the problem of causality, we have nearly lost sight of our original question of reality. This is not a matter of chance. In the thinkers we have discussed, the question of reality is shifted more and more to the question of what the *cause* of reality is. The cause has more reality than its effect, it is responsible for that effect, and it is what *reason* looks for to *explain* that effect and make it intelligible (explicable).

Kant's critical framework, which is of a wider scope than his Newtonian framework which has been justly criticized by subsequent thinkers as a perhaps inevitable limitation of his time, already determines from the outset what can qualify as real. What is real is quite simply what is *given* in experience. "Thoughts without content are empty, intuitions without concepts are blind."[35] "The understanding cannot see, the senses cannot think." (ibid) Experience by definition for Kant must always and without exception contain the two basic factors of sense intuition, the receptivity of sensibility, and of concepts ordering these intuitions, the spontaneity of the understanding. Thus what is real is what can actually be experienced, not merely thought, and in a closer analysis of the distinction between being known (experienced) and merely thought, the emphasis comes to rest upon the factor of *givenness* in sense intuition. In section III of the "System of the Principles of the Pure Understanding"[36] Kant gives a table of principles, i.e. rules for the objective use of the categories. The second principle, the anticipations of perception, grapples with the question of the real (*Realität*, not

Wirklichkeit,) the real in the sense yielded by a very technical breakdown of the components of experience, not in the more global and for us more important sense of reality as, say, opposed to unreality. (The opposite of reality in this section of the *Critique* is *negation*, not unreality.) The second principle refers to the second category, that of quality. We shall attempt to understand this perhaps least readily comprehensible of the categories and examine how it relates to the real, to time and to causality.

Anticipations of Perception

[The principle which anticipates all perception as such, is this: In all phenomena sensation, and the Real which corresponds to it in the object (*realitas phenomenon*), has an intensive quantity, *that is, a degree*]

Their principle is: In all phenomena the Real, which is the object of a sensation, has intensive quantity, that is, a degree.[37]

Whereas the first of the categories has to do with *extensive* quantity, the second deals with *intensive* quantity (*Grösse*), or degree. Extensive quantity refers to the fact that every phenomenon can be apprehended only by successively synthesizing the parts of the whole. Kant's first example here is that of representing a line to oneself. One cannot visualize a line in thought without, so to speak, constructing that line starting from a given point and producing all its parts. One does not perceive the line, as a line, instantaneously, but must go through the process of drawing it in thought.

What, then, is intensive quantity? Whereas the concept of extensive quantity gives us the notion of extension in general, intensive quantity gives us, so to speak, the "density" of our sense experience. Taking the simple example of a red apple, I perceive not only its size (extensive quantity), but also the degree of its redness, and that is its intensive quantity. The perception of intensive quantity is not a matter of piecing parts together, but of determining in a given perception *how* red, *how* warm, etc. (*quale*) it is. Intensive quantity corresponds to what Kant means here by reality. The anticipations of perception show that what is *a priori* in perception is 1) its necessary continuity and 2) the fact that it must have a degree of intensity, but not that actual degree itself which must be given in experience. We cannot perceive nothing, empty space or empty time; we cannot perceive a lack of reality. Thus what is *a posteriori* in experience is the real of sensation, the irreducible givenness filling time (and space). In the chapter on the schematism of the pure concepts of the understanding, Kant defines reality as what fills time to a greater or lesser degree. What corresponds in phenomena to sensation "constitutes the transcendental matter of all objects, as things in themselves (reality, *Sachheit*)." The real in this technical sense is the given (in sensation). All of our *a priori* faculties by themselves could never produce an experience of something real.

Now perception alone is not sufficient to determine the objective relation of phenomena. The apprehension of the manifold of phenomena is always successive, always in time. My apprehension, for example, of a house must take place in time in that I look at its various parts, sides etc. But that succession has no objective order, i.e. no order referring to the actual house itself. I can look at that house from left to right, up and down, but all of this has nothing to do with the house, rather with my subjective apprehension alone. The manifold of phenomena is always produced by the mind successively, whether the succession refers to an objective order in phenomena (not in things in themselves) or not, as in the case of the house. If, then, the experience in question involves not the apprehension of an object (house), but of events, some objective order must be present in the events in order to establish succession *in them*, and not just in our imagination or subjective experience. Otherwise the order of experience would be arbitrary as it is in a dream. I could only state that one (subjective) apprehension follows another, but never that two (objective) states follow each other in a phenomenon.

As Hume showed, if the connection of two states is derived empirically from experience, one is not justified in speaking of a necessary connection, or causality, but only of an observed conjunction which unthinking habit eventually congeals into a pseudo principle of "causality." Thus Kant, if he wished to establish the universality and necessity of the principle of causality, must show its *a priori* character, show that it is not derived empirically from experience, but precedes that experience and first makes it possible. Thus "we" put the rule of causality "into" experience, but if we did not, all of our experience would be dream experience, not experience of a given object or a series of events in objects. Kant states "We never . . . ascribe the sequence or consequence (of an event or something happening that did not exist before) to the object, and distinguish it from the subjective sequence of our apprehension, except when there is a rule which *forces* (nötigt) us to observe a certain order of perceptions, and no other; nay, that it is this force (Nötigung) which from the first renders the representation of a succession in the object possible.³⁸ Thus when it is a matter of objective phenomena, and not just imagination, the phenomenon is represented as an event, as something which happens, and this has a certain position in time which, after the preceding state, cannot be different from what it is. Kant concludes two things: 1) I cannot invert the order of these events (here, on the level of causality, or the connection of events in time, the essential irreversibility of time becomes apparent in a way absent from Kant's analysis of time as a form of pure sensibility) and 2) whenever the antecedent state is there, the other event must follow necessarily.

The experience that something happens becomes "real" when I consider the phenomenon as determined with regard to its place in time. The rule for determining everything according to the succession in time is that the condition under which an event follows necessarily is to be found in what precedes, and this rule is "the principle of sufficient reason." The empirical application of the pure concept of causality as a principle is ultimately made possible by means of the transcendental unity of apperception, the necessary connection of all consciousness in one original apperception. It is this self-contained unity which makes all experience *my* (coherent) experience, and not phantasies belonging to no one.

What has this digression into Kant's technical analysis of causality and the real accomplished? It has attempted to show the intimate connection, rather inscrutable in its ultimate implications, of the necessary *givenness* of the real (in sense intuition) with the *a priori* character of causality referring to an objective order of events to time in general. It is perhaps best for now not to force far-reaching conclusions from the relation of these three, conclusions which we are not now able to formulate and can perhaps never formulate with any triumphant degree of satisfaction. Once one leaves the relatively clear analyses of consciousness of a Descartes or a Hume and enters the field of German Idealism, critical and absolute, consciousness becomes a problem formidable in its intricacies. One is happy to *follow* the analyses, let alone get beyond them to some even more transcendental point of view. An analysis of consciousness on this level of philosophizing is a monumental task, a task perhaps pushed to the limits of its complexity by Edmund Husserl.

For our purposes now it is sufficient to say that Kant has here shown the absolutely necessary character of experience ordered by objective causality related to the givenness in sense intuition of the real in time. In other words, he has deduced (in his sense of the word deduction) a form of causality which is more or less "mechanistic" in its implications. The question then becomes: how is causality through freedom (teleology) possible.?

This question, of course, belongs preeminently to the third Critique, the "synthesis" of the Critique of Pure and of Practical Reason. Again, we can only touch upon some of the questions dealt with in this formidable work. But some discussion of them, however sketchy and superficial, is necessary for our purposes. One cannot get to the culmination of the identification of the real and the rational with Hegel—which will conclude our investigation of this relation—without considering Kant.

Toward the end of the *Critique of Pure Reason* Kant asks the three questions focussing the whole *interest*, speculative and practical, of reason.

1. What can I know?
2. What should I do?
3. What may I hope?

These three questions constitute the single question: what is man? The practical interest of reason boils down to two questions: Is there a God? Is there a future life? These questions have to do with practical freedom which we know by experience as a causality of reason determining the will. They involve *moral* freedom, not transcendental freedom which has to do with the *absolute* causality of reason independent of the conditions of (sense) experience, a question which speculative reason cannot answer. The *a priori* principle of the understanding is conformity to law and its realm of application is nature. The *a priori* principle of reason is final purpose and its realm of application is freedom. Between these two, understanding related to nature and reason related to freedom, lies the judgment whose *a priori* principle is purposiveness and whose realm of application is art. It is the judgment which is to effect a kind of transition from nature to freedom, to link the understanding with reason. Judgment can be either determinative or reflective. A determinative judgment, by far the most familiar and common kind, subsumes the particular under the universal. Reflective judgment, on the other hand, starts with a given particular and looks for the corresponding universal. This reflective judgment requires an *a priori* principle in order to find the universal which it seeks, a principle which it cannot borrow from experience because the universal in question is not given to it. But neither can the reflective judgment prescribe this principle to nature since it would then put an end to its search by imposing its own conditions on nature and these conditions concern only the possibility of nature (nature defined as the totality of appearances) in general. They cannot explain an order or a systematic unity of particular, empirical rules. In short, the principle which the reflective judgment requires can neither be found in nature nor prescribed to it. Kant defines this principle as follows:

> As universal laws of nature have their ground in our understanding, which prescribes them to nature, (although only according to the universal concept of it as nature), so particular empirical laws, in respect of what is in them left undetermined by those universal laws, must be considered in accordance with such a unity as they would have if an understanding (although

not our understanding) had furnished them to our cognitive faculties, so as to make possible a system of experience according to the particular laws of nature.[39]

The principle of judgment is thus the purposiveness of nature in its variety. This principle represents nature as if an understanding, though not our own, contained the ground of the unity of the variety of its empirical laws. These particular empirical laws are far too various to conform to the *a priori* laws of our understanding, and yet they exhibit a purposiveness which indicates ultimately for Kant that they are only comprehensible in terms of a design. And this purposive design which the reflective judgment seeks but can never cognize objectively as a purpose must be the product and intention of a divine intellect, an *intellectus archetypus*. No design can be ascribed to inanimate matter. Thus purposiveness is incomprehensible to us unless it refers beyond the determined, mechanical nexus of efficient causes to what Kant repeatedly throughout all three critiques calls a supersensible substrate, in this case God.

One can see how far removed Kant is here from either an Aristotle or a Spinoza. For Aristotle, an organized living being had its purpose (*telos*) within itself; it had no need of a being external to it to give it its design. The whole concept of *entelecheia*, having the end in oneself, is quite foreign to what Kant is aiming at here. And on the other hand, Spinoza, who rejects final causes in general, regards the attribution of final purposes to God as a kind of anthropomorphic arrogance. The arrogance is not diminished, but rather entrenched by appealing to the (unknowable) will of God for what cannot quite be explained, i.e. to the asylum of ignorance, as Spinoza calls it.

But for Kant purposiveness is flatly incomprehensible without an intelligence behind it, a world designer who cannot be trapped and ensnared within the causality of phenomena. One can appreciate this feeling about purposiveness which, if it does not root itself in the realm of morality and produce a sense of admiration, can easily seem downright uncanny. Apart from viewing the world as created expressly for the benefit of man, a view to which catastrophes and apparently senseless suffering belong as the counterphenomenon of punishing man for his sins and misdeeds, one can still look upon the amazing coherence of life, for example, the fact that an embryo actually grows into an infant if nothing "interferes from outside"—Aristotle's *tyraten*—, and wonder how this is possible. This wonder may stop short of positing a guiding intelligence, and yet it can lead to asking the question: Why is there anything at all? without being able or even wanting to give Leibniz' answer to this question. The question admits of no answer, and an answer is not the meaning of the question. The question leads us into the dizzying vortex of trying to imagine a beginning of the world, or no beginning at all—which is perhaps even more staggering if one persists in trying to do this. The complacent theories of evolution do not obviate this dilemma—Where did the primordial slime or the cataclysms of exploding masses of matter come from? And so on. This kind of wonder is, so to speak, the external counterpart of the root-shaking experience common to many children and to thinking beings still capable of wonder, namely the question: Who am I? This question has no answer either. Again, the meaning of this question lies not in an answer, but in persisting in this question and *experiencing* it.

In the dialectic of the teleological judgment, Kant formulates the antinomy of mechanical and final causality. It is indeed an antinomy, i.e. the two kinds cannot ultimately coexist side by side as they could for Leibniz, nor can one be derived from the other, but they must rather somehow ultimately be reconciled in a higher ground.

> The first maxim of judgment is the *proposition*: all production of material things and their forms must be judged to be possible according to merely mechanical laws.
>
> The second maxim is the *counterposition*: some products of material nature cannot be judged to be possible according to merely mechanical laws. (To judge them requires a different law of causality, namely, that of final causes.)
>
> If these regulative principles of investigation be converted into constitutive principles of the possibility of objects, they will run thus:
>
> *Proposition*: All production of material things is possible according to merely mechanical laws.

Counterposition: Some production of material things is not possible according to merely mechanical laws.[40]

How and to what extent does Kant reconcile this antinomy? By appealing to his fundamental tenet of the distinction between phenomena and noumena. Causality of nature applies to phenomena, causality of freedom applies to noumena. Thus the "conflict" between the two mutually exclusive kinds of causality is anchored in that distinction and is ultimately reducible to it.

One of the various pretended contradictions in this whole distinction of the causality of nature from that of freedom is this. It is objected that, if I speak of *obstacles* which nature opposes to causality according to (moral) laws of freedom or of the *assistance* it affords, I am admitting an *influence* of the former upon the latter. But if we try to understand what has been said, this misinterpretation is very easy to avoid. The opposition or assistance is not between nature and freedom, but between the former as phenomenon and the effects of the latter as phenomenon in the world of sense. The causality of freedom itself (of pure and practical reason) is the causality of a natural cause subordinated to nature (i.e. of the subject considered as a man, and therefore as phenomenon). The intelligible, which is thought under freedom, contains the ground of the *determination* of this (natural cause) in a further inexplicable way (just as that intelligible does which constitutes the supersensible substrate of nature).[41]

Thus Kant concludes that reason possesses causality not with regard to the laws of nature—for then our will could directly affect natural occurrences; if I were furious at someone, I could, for example, conjure up a mighty thunderstorm to express my anger dramatically—but with regard to free actions within the framework of nature.[42] The most immediate problem we are left with here is the extent of the freedom of our actions. Kant gives the example that if he wants to get up from his chair, he can do so and thus originate a new series of events not determined by preceding ones. This seems to present no problem. But in more crucial situations the question of freedom becomes more acute. An ill man cannot simply will to recover from his illness if the causality of nature has started some irreversible and progressive disease in his body. Everyone is probably aware of a delicate balance here between "nature" (mechanism in the broadest sense possible, i.e., causality with no relation to a free, thinking being) and freedom. Many of the questions of daily life are bound up with the limitation of our freedom by external circumstances, other people, etc. and make us ask *why* this limitation of our freedom. Why does someone become incurably schizophrenic, why does someone get run over in an automobile accident, why does a composer become deaf (Beethoven) or become utterly unable to produce music? (The problem portrayed in Thomas Mann's *Dr. Faustus*.) The "answers" to these questions are no answers at all. They refer to the inexorable causality of nature, the inexorable network of circumstances meshing together to produce a situation. There is no intentionality in most of these situations there is no reason why.

All of this by no means denies freedom, but merely shows its intrinsically problematic character. Kant is left with the division of phenomena and noumena and with the problem of their possible interaction. Of the three Ideas of reason, God, freedom and immortality, it is freedom alone which is "the only concept of the supersensible which (by means of the causality that is thought in it) proves its objective reality in nature by means of the effects it can produce there, and thus renders possible the connection of both the others with nature and of all three together with religion."[43]

Freedom is to effect the "synthesis" between the phenomenal and the noumenal realms. Freedom is inexplicable in terms of the order of nature and yet it is empirically real; we have concrete evidence of its actuality. This is as far as Kant can go. *How* that freedom is possible, how it operates we can never know. For one thing, it would be inadmissable to relate the two realms by means of causality, a category of the pure understanding and applicable only to phenomena. Since our intuition is always only an intuition of sense (never intellectual intuition)[42] and since our understanding is always only discursive, never intuitive, our knowledge constituted by these two faculties can never know anything but phenomena. Kant never relinquished this basic position. It remained for Hegel to do so.

Hegel is the last and culminating figure in our stroll through rationalism. He threw Kant's caution to the winds and abolished the distinction between phenomena and noumena. It is the noumenon, the thing in itself, which *appears*. A distinction or a discrepancy between reality and appearance is impossible, even senseless. And what appears, what *is*, is not only comprehensible for reason, it *is* Reason. Thus the well known sentence from the preface to the *Philosophy of Law*:

The rational is the real
And the real is the rational.

And further:

To comprehend *what is* is the task of philosophy, for *what is*, is reason.

In the first quote the real (*was wirklich ist*) is sometimes translated as the actual. This is misleading because it fails to see the *exclusive* character of what Hegel means by the real. The opposite of the actual is the possible or better the potential, what has not yet been actualized. This puts the meaning of the actual in the framework of modality, possibility and "reality" in the sense of the actual. But that is not what Hegel is talking about. The opposite of the real for Hegel is the *unreal* which is ultimately what is inessential and/or partial. The real *excludes* the "unreal" if the latter is inessential; it *incorporates* (hebt auf) the "unreal" if it is a partial reality. The unreal is either a not or, more often, a not yet. If one objected to Hegel that something irrational is, after all, real, he can reply: so much the worse for the real. In other words, if it is not rational, it is not *real*.

In concluding this chapter on the role of reason in relation to reality, we want to see what happens to the other cognitive— not the non-rational—faculties as compared with reason. This involves Hegel's rejection of Kant, and in a different way Fichte and Schelling. Finally, what more or less corresponds to "causality" in Hegel is the structure of his dialectic, and this we want to examine briefly.

Hegel has no use for intuition as a means of knowing what is ultimately real, neither sense intuition nor—Absolute Spirit forbid—intellectual intuition. The sense intuition which Kant so tenaciously held on to as the *conditio sine qua non* of knowledge as opposed to merely thinking something is blithely relegated by Hegel to the realm of the mere particular. Sense intuition is at best the stage of immediacy and bare generality. Hegel polemicizes against any kind of immediacy giving essential knowledge since mediation is precisely the function of the dialectic and the "truth" is the *result* of this dialectic. The "truth" is result, the truth is the (mediated) whole.

As criteria for essential knowledge, Hegel rejects: 1) sense intuition (Kant) as inadequate; 2) intellectual intuition (Schelling) as impossible and muddle-headed; 3) thinking in figurative ideas (*Vorstellungen*) which is bound by habit to *material* images; 4) *formal* intelligence (*raisonnement*) which merely rambles about, gets nowhere, and cannot grasp (*begreifen*) its content; 5) instinctive, imaginative, revelatory inspiration, neither poetry nor philosophy, a production of "jejeune prose" or, at best, "raving nonsense"; 6) common sense; and 7) the ego and moral action (Fichte), the ought as opposed to the is, and so on with many polemical subdivisions.

We shall focus our discussion of Hegel on two factors. First we shall speak about the kinds of knowledge just listed which Hegel rejects in order to see the nature of his claim for reason, the concept (*Begriff*), the Idea. This survey can be fruitful in that it offers a panorama of the human faculties which serves to make the "rational" more concrete and to point out its unique character. Then we shall make the difficult attempt to analyze the structure of his dialectic, not just by quoting the familiar triadic in itself, for itself, in and for itself, but by trying to see how that structure generates actual *occurrence* out of itself.

We shall abandon the haphazard order of our list and try to simplify the basic targets of Hegel's polemic. Hegel's polemic has two basic levels. One level is the relatively non-philosophical one of common sense, "feeling" and mathematical reasoning.

This non-philosophical level is, of course, operative in the philosopher too, since he thinks like anyone else prior to his philosophical reflection and, to the extent that he is subject to habit, always thinks like anyone else. The other level is the philosophical one, and on this level Hegel is in constant dialogue with his contemporaries Fichte and Schelling and his immediate predecessor Kant. This dialogue centers on the problem of intuition. There is a sense in which what a thinker combats and objects to is most instructive for what he himself wants to say, a sense in which all polemic is a kind of "negative theology."

To take the non-philosophical level first, we have, of course, common sense against which philosophers have polemicized as long as there have been philosophers (cf. Heraclitus). Hegel has the very specific objection to the common sense attitude that it takes contradiction as something final. It stops short before the contradiction of opposites and declares them both false. Common sense is incapable of seeing that contradiction and negation are at the very heart of things, that they are not in static opposition, but move and constitute the very movement of life. Perhaps the prime instance of common sense is its habit of thinking in figurative ideas (*Vorstellungen*), a habit which confines it to what is material. The opposite of this kind of thinking is what Hegel calls *raisonnement*, purely formal thinking detached from all content. Both kinds of thinking are one-sided, the merely material and the other merely formal. But the latter kind rather belongs to the discussion of the philosophical level.

Hegel attacks mathematical thinking for much the same reason, that it deals with static elements and is unable to comprehend the factor of movement. The principle of mathematics is quantity. Thus for Hegel it deals with abstract unrealities lacking self-movement and unable to comprehend time as time. But since time is the concept itself in the form of existence,[45] if mathematics cannot deal with time, it is very definitely on the outside of things. It cannot deal with "the sheer restlessness of life." It is at best, so to speak, the paralyzed surface of the Absolute. Much of this attack on mathematical thinking is aimed at Spinoza's *Ethics*, but really concerns only Spinoza's manner of presentation. One can hardly call Spinoza's thinking "mathematical" in its core. How could a mathematician get to intellectual intuition or the intellectual love of God (unless he were an Einstein)?

Finally, there is feeling. If common sense leaves things standing side by side and if mathematical thinking stays on the outside of things, feeling jumps right in and revels in an ecstatic enthusiasm in the oneness of things. Hegel distrusts and pours scorn on the man of feeling, "God's beloved one to whom he gives His wisdom in sleep" (*Phenomenology*, Preface). Feeling cannot arrive at a direct knowledge of the Absolute (no such knowledge is possible or desirable according to Hegel), but rather belongs to animal life. "What is anti-human, the condition of mere animals, consists in keeping within the sphere of feeling pure and simple, and in being able to communicate only by way of feeling-states."[46] We shall encounter this polemic against feeling again in the instance of Schelling on the level of philosophical objections to which we now turn.

Hegel has a multitude of objections to Kant's treatment of the two fundamental constituents of experience, the categories and intuition. If, as Kant insists, the categories belong ineluctably to the *finite* mind, they can never lead to a knowledge of the Absolute.[47] Since Hegel abolishes the most basic distinction of Kant's philosophy, its very ontological foundation, the distinction between appearances and things in themselves, the categories are for him no longer finite. They are not only applicable to the Absolute, they are the positive determinations of the Absolute appearing in history. For Hegel, the *thing-in-itself appears*, which means ultimately that it is meaningless to speak of the thing-*in-itself*. It has become a useless and superfluous concept.

Furthermore, the categories, or thinking in general, cannot be restricted in their application to sense intuition because this sense intuition is nothing ultimate and self-sufficient. Thus for Hegel the concepts should not be conditioned by mere matter— in which case they would have to remain finite—they transform that matter and elevate it to their own element of thought. If thinking and appearances don't correspond, why should the fault lie with thinking? In the choice between thinking and intuition Hegel very definitely opts for thinking. Sense intuition is no longer the ballast anchoring us in a level of experience beneath that of the concept or the absolute Idea. To maintain the Kantian position is to get stranded in a very partial reality, to abort the process of development from the fragmented concrete particular to the unified concrete universal.

> To think the empirical world means essentially rather to change its empirical form and transform it into something universal. Thinking exercises at the same time a *negative* activity on that foundation. When the material (*Stoff*) perceived is determined by universality, it *does not remain in its empirical form.*[48]

Thought and intuition do not remain side by side in ongoing experience. Rather, thought supersedes (*hebt auf*) intuition; it transforms the particular element of immediate sense perception into the universal mediated element of thought. The words *Aufheben,* 'mediation,' 'dialectic' all indicate the activity of thinking and thus the character of the world process since this process is the manifestation of Absolute Spirit. Hegel claims that the nature of this activity is such that it can bridge the gap between sense intuition and thought and also the gap between the finite and the infinite. He does not sanction the hallowed chasm upheld by most previous thinkers between a causally connected chain of finite beings and the infinite which cannot be comprehended in this chain, but is at best to be grasped at by the process of analogy. No, for Hegel the very nature of the finite is to supersede itself, and in so doing it is on its way to the infinite. To know that we are limited means for Hegel to be conscious of the real presence of the infinite.[49]

All of these remarks and criticisms point to dialectic as the crux of Hegel's position. Before turning to that difficult subject, we first want to finish the discussion of intuition, proceeding to the critique of *intellectual* intuition. The German Idealist thinkers all share an admiration for Spinoza, particularly for his conception of a "system," of the comprehensive vision of God and the world which they embraced with enthusiasm. Their *critique* of Spinoza was that he conceived the Absolute as substance, a substance which they found static and lifeless. The Idealist thinkers conceived of the Absolute as *subject,* and their central concern became the problem of absolute subjectivity.

Instead of Spinoza's substance which had an infinite number of attributes, two of which were known to man, i.e. extension and thinking, the Idealists in general posited "reality" in the absolute Ego, the absolute Spirit or subject, and pondered the ramifications of somehow deriving the objective world from that subjective reality. The problem for them then became which faculty of absolute subjectivity or Spirit is the highest or most fundamental one. For Fichte this faculty was the activity of the absolute Ego, the positing of itself and of a non-ego. Fichte's basic principle was the self-certainty of the absolute Ego obtained in an intellectual intuition of itself. Schelling, who went through manifold stages of development, also asserted throughout most of those stages intellectual intuition as an immediate unity of the philosopher with the Absolute to be the highest principle. It was Hegel whose Absolute was the very overcoming (Aufhebung) of immediacy in the mediating activity of the concept (*Begriff*). Thus from Hegel's standpoint intellectual intuition could never yield ultimate knowledge of the Absolute. It could at best be a preliminary point of departure, but never commensurate with absolute Spirit whose very nature was dialectical mediation.

Thus the divergent problematic of the German Idealists among themselves boils down to the question of immediacy versus mediation. We shall pursue Hegel's critique of intellectual intuition, in which he mostly had Schelling in mind, and then proceed to Hegel's own concept of reality as the peak of "rationalism." The difficulty now will be not to get lost in the somewhat incredible intricacies of these thinkers. They were struggling with the extremely difficult subject of thinking itself on a level of philosophical sophistication and acumen seldom attained by thinkers before or after them. Even if post-Idealist philosophy cannot return to the position of absolute Idealism, it should acknowledge the rather magnificent attempt to discuss a problem which cannot be ignored by modern philosophy after Descartes, namely, the problem of *mediation*, the problem of how the mind comes to its experience. It is not possible or philosophically tenable to exempt completely the post-Idealist thinkers such as Nietzsche or Kierkegaard from the criticism that they simply ignore or reject the question of mediation under the banner of "Life" or "the existing individual."

Hegel's critique of Schelling is quite acrid and approaches hilarity in its scorn of all immediacy. For Hegel, immediacy is a brand of formalism, a formalism unable to penetrate and grasp its "material." Formalism remains of necessity outside of its content. It cannot "do anything" with that content, but rather falls into circular, empty assertions which fail to explain or mediate anything at all. The phrase "all animals," says Hegel, cannot pass for zoology. It does not tell us anything, although formally it appears to make some kind of comprehensive statement. The same thing applies to more formally articulated statements such as "God is One," "God is eternal." They do not tell us anything about God. The situation takes a turn for the ludicrous when Hegel, parodying Schelling, pokes fun at statements which, under the guise of a feeble kind of analogy, merely equate things which cannot be brought together in any simple way. "Formalism in the case of speculative Philosophy of Nature (*Naturphilosophie*) takes the shape of teaching that understanding is electricity, animals are nitrogen, or equivalent to south or north and so on."[50] Statements such as these are for Hegel the result of the "pigeon-hole process" of the understanding. They yield a *table* of contents, but no content. They classify or equate, they do not mediate.

The claim for immediacy is "the sort of ecstatic enthusiasm which starts straight off with absolute knowledge as if shot out of a pistol." And this absolute knowledge lands us in the proverbial night in which alls cows are black, i.e. we are very much One with the Absolute but also very much in the dark.

What is the gist of all this polemic against intellectual intuition, against immediacy? Whatever is immediate lacks the "power of the negative." Without the power of the negative, immediate knowledge for Hegel probably amounts to a kind of naive, spurious sense-consciousness. The immediacy of formalism cannot be the same principle taking shape in truly diverse ways (Hegel), but is merely the shapeless repetition of the same idea, applied in external fashion to different matter. This principle never gets anywhere, but simply falls back upon itself again and again in the circular manner which was the bane of these Idealists. Unlike previous thinkers, the Idealists are not asking "what" the Absolute "is," but rather about its *activity*. And this makes the question "what does it do," "where does it take us" supreme. For Hegel, this activity is self-identity re-instating itself in otherness. Otherness necessarily involves negation, a negation which truly transposes immediate identity out of itself without losing its essential nature.

Thus for Hegel, more than for the other Idealists, the Absolute is to be conceived as a "System" not only in the sense that everything is to be understood in its interconnectedness and "standing together" (*systema*), but above all in its progressive development toward a final result containing everything essential. The truth is the whole, the Absolute is essentially a *result*.

If the nature of reality lies in absolute subjectivity, the question of which faculty of subjectivity expresses what is most real finds its answer in reason, reason conceived as dialectical mediation. The real is the rational and the rational is the real. This statement represents the culmination of the long development in its Western tradition beginning with Plato. The sense realm, however, is not separated here from the realm of reason, but is incorporated and transformed by reason. Nothing can be left standing alone and separate for Hegel, without being devoured by the mediating process of the concept. The "reason" which is real here is not "our" reason searching for reasons why. It *is* living reason itself, it *is* the Absolute. Thus the questions of causality which concerned us throughout much of this chapter now become submerged. Causality no longer has to do with our manner of explanation of the nature of the world. Mechanism and teleology are stages of development on the way toward the most comprehensive kind of causality of all, reciprocal causality (*Wechselwirkung*). What is important here is not so much the dialectical progression of these kinds of causality, but rather the fact that they are no longer questions about the nature of the world. They claim to describe facets or "moments" of the development of the Absolute. The Absolute is not primarily the "reason why" for the world, its transcendent creator. Rather, the world process is the manifestation of the Absolute itself. The German Idealists could never have taken this step without

Spinoza who completely rejected, not so much any transcendence of the Absolute (this is a complex question and concerns the problem of "pantheism"), but rather creation.

The relation of reason and reality proclaimed by Hegel is no longer that of the Greeks. Reason is no longer that which gives us *access to* reality, it *is* Reality with a capital R, i.e. *absolute* Reality. Reason is no longer the *finite* reason of man. There is no place in Hegel for any ultimacy of finitude. The reason which Hegel is talking about is absolute Reason. It remained for later thinkers to take human finitude seriously as something which cannot be *aufgehoben* and overcome. Together with the realization of the centrality of finitude goes the realization that reason no longer even takes us to the Absolute (the later Schelling). The centrality of finitude led to the insight that the categories of the finite mind do not lead to the Absolute.

CHAPTER 2

The Non-Rational Faculties within the Framework of Rationalism

W hereas a development took place in the conception of reason from Plato to Hegel, a development consisting in the increasing subjectification of reason, no such development is to be found for the non-rational faculties. The non-rational faculties—emotions, feelings, desires etc.—were considered subjective to begin with. They did not furnish any kind of "objective" knowledge, but were on the whole rather something to be controlled, even guarded against. That aspect of the non-rational faculties was touched upon in the first chapter in the discussion of Plato. This chapter will briefly discuss Aristotle's treatment of the emotions in the *Rhetoric*, and then go on to the seventeenth century rationalists who, precisely because they were rationalists, were forced to examine and come to terms with the emotions. They were preoccupied with them.

It is significant that Aristotle's discussion of the emotions takes place within the context of the *Rhetoric*.[1] Thus, apart from the *Poetics* where he discusses the *function* of tragedy in purifying us of pity and fear, the emotions are being analyzed in order to find out how to arouse them in the listener. Aristotle begins by asking what the causes of an action are, for example, why would a defendant commit a crime? He lists seven causes of action: chance, nature, compulsion, habit, reasoning (rational craving), anger or appetite (irrational craving). A man's action is either due to himself or not due to himself. To say that a man's action is due to himself is tantamount to saying that he is responsible for that action. In the first three instances cited I am not the cause of an action. If a stone falls on my head by chance or if an acorn grows into an oak tree by nature, there is no agency on my part involved. Aristotle's third factor, compulsion, is more controversial, particularly when considered in the light of the findings of modern psychology. Aristotle does not equate it with the sixth factor, irrational craving; for the person with a compulsion to do something does not crave or even wish to do it. Action done under compulsion "takes place contrary to the desire or reason of the doer, yet through his own agency."[2] Compulsion seems to be even less comprehensible than blind irrational desire, for that desiring person at least *wants* what he desires even if attainment is detrimental to him. Without saying very much about it, Aristotle has discovered a strange force in man which goes against both his reason *and* his desire and over which he has little or no control.

The sixth factor, habit, shares with compulsion its repetetive nature, but it is a more benificent force and it is, at least initially, under our control. Habit is akin to nature in its uniformity; and, in fact, is a kind of "second" nature which we acquire to facilitate things for ourselves. Perhaps one of the most strenuous and exhausting things about new and strange situations is that there is no habit to fall back and rely upon. Everything must be done in terms of conscious choice and decision. Considered by itself and out of a context, habit is a "neutral" factor rooted in past experience. It can be negative, as in the case of bad habits which we try to "break." Less dramatically and obviously but also more pervasively and insidiously, it is habit which in the long run dulls the intensity of our experience, and leads to boredom and a kind of blind habituation incapable of feeling. Finally, habits can be beneficial by taking the burden of constant decisions from us. They then approach something like an acquired "instinct."

In conclusion, Aristotle discusses rational and irrational desires. Irrational desires could be contrary to reason, but they could also be "natural" desires such as thirst and hunger; whereas rational desires arise from an opinion held by the mind. Actions motivated by rational desires are either ends or means to an end. They have a "reason why" and aim at what is useful or good or at least pleasant.

After analyzing these motives for action, Aristotle goes on to define an emotion. First, however, he must define pleasure and pain since emotions are to be considered as either pleasant or painful, as "positive" or "negative." "Pleasure is a movement, a movement by which the soul as a whole is consciously brought into its normal state of being; pain is the opposite."[3] What is perhaps most interesting about this comprehensive definition of pleasure and pain is that they are not *states*, but *transitions*, movements; thus bringing them close to the idea of emotion in its etymological sense of what *moves*, effects a change. "The emotions are all those feelings that so change men as to affect their judgments, and that are also attended by pain or pleasure."[4] This might be rephrased as follows: Emotions are conscious transitions from one state of being to another, and they are either pleasant or painful. This is about as far as Aristotle takes us in the *Rhetoric*, for his primary aim is not so much an analysis of emotion as such, but rather how to *arouse* the emotions in the framework of persuading an audience by means of rhetoric. Thus he stipulates that in order to induce, for example, anger effectively in an audience, one must know three things, i.e., (1) what the state of mind of angry people is; (2) who the people are with whom they usually get angry; and (3) on what grounds they get angry with them. This is interesting and not irrelevant to our inquiry into the non-rational faculties, but to go into it in detail would be a kind of detour which we can avoid. The remainder of the *Rhetoric*, which is more central for us, consists in a classification of the emotions, mostly in pairs of opposites such as anger-calm, friendship-enmity, etc. with a few emotions which have no opposite, i.e., envy. This kind of classification is later epitomized by Spinoza. Finally, Aristotle enumerates the contributing factors related to human character. In addition to the emotions, there are moral qualities (virtues and vices), the factor of age (youth, prime of life and old age), and fortune (birth, wealth, power and their opposites). In other words, man's inclination to be moral or immoral plays a part in the development of his total character as do the time of his

life in which he stands and also the kind of favorable or un-
favorable situation in which he happens to be. All of these
factors have an "influence" on human character. What Aristotle
implies but does not quite specify is that the emotions also
influence character. We are left somewhat up in the air as to
whether these emotions are "products" of situations or whether
they do not perhaps themselves influence situations. This ambiguity is the beginning of the long controversy whether emotions are merely reactions to situations or whether they help
determine those situations, a controversy which, among other
possibilities, lands in modern psychology's *aporia* of heredity
versus environment. In the constantly recurring phrases "state
of mind," "frame of mind," Aristotle approaches a phenomenon
for which we have at this stage of our inquiry no adequate
language, something akin to "temperament." It is impossible to
say much that is conclusive at this point unless we force Aristotle
beyond himself. The framework of his express aim of inquiry,
how to arouse emotion by means of rhetoric, prohibits him from
probing the question of the *meaning* of emotion. We shall return
to this question later. We are, of course, "begging the question,"
but as that most honest of all philosophers, Spinoza, once re-
marked: "nor can I explain this more clearly at present."

On our way to Spinoza who is the thinker to treat the
emotions most comprehensively and systematically after Aristotle, we should mention in passing Galen, and then Descartes.
Again, this is not a matter of historical development as it was
in the case of reason. The problem of the non-rational faculties,
and that means for the rationalists the emotions, never gets
developed. The emotions remain as a static, problematical if
not actually suspect quasi-area of the human being. Various
possibilities are explored within this area, but the area itself and
the kind of questioning remain the same.

The thinker and physician Claudius Galenus (131 A.D.) is
worthy of mention in our inquiry because, following Hippo-
crates, he formulated the now familiar theory of the "four temperaments": the melancholic, the choleric, the sanguine and the
phlegmatic temperaments. It was Galen's insight that different
kinds of "temperament" distinguish different kinds of human
beings. Temperament has little to do with reasoning or intelli-

gence, nor can it be reductively attributed to a collection of expressions of emotion. On the contrary, temperament, or the way man is tempered or attuned to the world, goes a long way toward explaining emotions, reactions, and a great deal else. As a physician, Galen found the explanation for the different temperaments in a predominance of some bodily substance, blood, phlegm, bile. What is interesting about his theory is not so much his emphasis on the body—which was natural for him and moreover cannot be ignored in this context, although it does not *explain* anything—but his insistence that "the genesis of these humours is accomplished in the body." In other words, temperament is a kind of *internal* principle not to be explained by nutrition or other environmental factors.

With Descartes philosophy in general is placed upon a new foundation, the *fundamentum inconcussum* of the "I think," and this new foundation cannot fail to have consequences for an understanding of the emotions. In contrast to Aristotle for whom the soul was the "form" or principle of the body, Descartes separates mind and body (or matter in general) so completely that they are tenuously held together only by the famous (or infamous) pineal gland. Thus, Descartes entitles his treatise on the emotions *Les Passions de l'ame*, the passions of the *soul*. Instead of having a middle faculty amenable to reason but not actually a rational faculty (as did Pascal and Aristotle), Descartes' analysis of the emotions shuttles back and forth between physiological description on the one hand and definition and classification of the various emotions on the other. He states at the beginning that what the ancients wrote on this subject was so slight and so far from credible that he feels he must start afresh, taking no account of those earlier writings. To recapitulate, Aristotle in a different context in his inquiry in the *Nichomachean Ethics* about what virtue is lists three states of soul as likely candidates for explaining the nature of virtue. These states are (1) an emotion; (2) a capacity; and (3) a disposition. Emotion he defines as a state of consciousness accompanied by pleasure or pain. Capacity is the faculty in virtue of which we can be said to be liable to the emotions; i.e., capable of feeling; for example, anger. Disposition is the formed state of character in virtue of which one is well- or ill-disposed in respect of the emotions. Aristotle concludes that whereas we are *moved* by the emotions, we are only *disposed* by virtue or vice. Disposition is temporally of "a longer range" and is acquired as a result of continually acting in a certain way. In contrast to actions which we can control from beginning to end, an emotion can be controlled only at its incipience. Once we are in the grasp of a strong emotion, there is very little we can do about it. Perhaps the most decisive characteristic of emotion throughout the philosophical tradition is that we are passive to it in the technical sense of undergoing it, being subject to it.

Now since for Descartes, the body is a mechanism, an extended thing which does not think, he must ask which functions belong to the body and which to the soul. A passion he defines as "all that which occurs or happens anew" with regard to the subject to which it occurs. Thus, everything which we experience in ourselves which can possibly exist in inanimate bodies must be attributed to our body alone. What cannot be conceived as pertaining to a body then belongs to the soul. Since the body cannot think, it is described physiologically in terms of heat, movement of the members, blood and animal spirits, which are strictly material. The soul does not supply this movement and heat as it implicitly did for Aristotle. The body is a self-contained mechanism. This is probably the source for Leibniz' criticism of mechanism that mechanical manipulation by itself could never produce a thought or even a sensation.[5] Thus, what in our experience is left for the soul are thoughts alone, some active (desires) and some passive (the perceptions which the soul receives from things). Both of these belong exclusively to the soul. The soul is active and in power over its desires, and passive and dependent upon the perceptions it receives from things. Descartes enumerates six primitive passions: wonder, love, hatred, desire, joy, sadness. Of these, wonder is unique in that, being related to knowledge alone, it is not accompanied by any bodily change, but solely related to the brain. The remaining passions are all either united or opposed to each other—whereas wonder has no opposite—and their "cause" lies in the body as well. Animal spirits act upon the pineal gland which in its turn brings about the passions of the soul.

We do not want to go into the obvious difficulties inherent

in Descartes' conception, but rather examine the general suppositions involved in order to see how the rationalist tradition formulates the question of the emotions. Our aim in this chapter and in this study in general is to try to see how "something" far more comprehensive and far-reaching in its implications and *meaning* than the "emotions" gets classified as these emotions, separated from reason and defined as "irrational" if not kept in "control." There is no such split of body and mind for Aristotle who conceives the soul's faculty as "pyramidal"; i.e., the being who possesses the highest faculty of reason, man, also includes the lower faculties of nutrition and sensation. Because of his drastic dualism, Descartes would have to say that the animal or brute was incapable of emotion which, with the exception of wonder in Descartes' list, is patently false.

What can we say about the analysis of the emotions at this point in order to gain some kind of foothold? The emotions or passions are something which have power over us and which we can control little or perhaps not at all. The practical function of reason is to moderate the intensity of this power which does not seem to come from "us." The power of these emotions or passions *moves* us to be in a certain "state" and also, according to Descartes, to desire to do something; i.e., the emotion of fear incites us to desire to flee.

Emotion, like the imagination, seems to be caught in the middle of two diametrically opposed faculties having little or nothing to do with each other. We shall take imagination first as the faculty more familiar in philosophical analysis, above all Kant's. Imagination is placed between reason and the senses. It shares with sense experience the fact that it has to do with sense images. But since these sense images are not produced by or reducible to an actually present sense object, they share with reason or thinking the fact that they are "abstract," present to thought alone. Similarly, emotions have something to do with the body and the senses (cf. for instance, Descartes' detailed analysis of facial expressions, breathing, pulse, etc), but also with the mind, since I must have some cognition of that emotion, otherwise I am talking about an abstracted reductivist physiology which merely calculates and measures bodily changes. The latter is certainly possible (witness the lie detector test), but utterly fails to comprehend anything of the power and richness of emotions such as love or hate. Indeed, it is often precisely a strong emotion which "brings something home" to me; i.e., makes me really understand something or someone or gain insight into them. One factor which emotion quite unambiguously shares with bodily senses is its *immediacy*. There is nothing discursive about feeling and emotion as there is in the process of reasoning something out. I have no "time" to consider whether to laugh or not. I simply laugh, immediately, perhaps even explosively.

To sum up at this point: emotions are something which overcome us, which we undergo. We cannot produce them at all or control them very effectively. Emotions are almost always analyzed as grouped in pairs, pleasant or painful. A pleasant emotion is *elevating*, a painful one *depressing*. We shall have the opportunity later on to question this seemingly unproblematic description of emotions in terms of being higher or lower. Finally, emotions inhabit different time spans, they can be volatile or quite durable. Revenge, for example, is an extremely durable emotion, whereas surpise is of necessity quite brief.

We turn now to Spinoza and Leibniz to finish this discussion of the non-rational faculties, termed the emotions, within the framework of rationalism. The role and function of the emotions in Spinoza is extremely complex, far richer and more intriguing than in the impoverished treatment by his predecessor, Descartes. There is also a great deal of fruitful and thought-provoking ambiguity as to the *meaning* of emotions for Spinoza, expressed in an oversimplified way as to the question of the "negative" or "affirmative" and "positive" character of the emotions in man's life. For a larger frame of reference than we are taking here; i.e., for Spinoza's thought as a whole, there are many problems more central than what we shall try to focus on; for instance, the mind-body problem. Whereas we certainly cannot *ignore* that problem, to go into it in its entirety and all its implications, would constitute a separate study. Again and again, in the thinkers selected for discussion in this study, the question of the emotions seems to involve us immediately in the whole of the thought in question. This is due, partly, to the "middle" or "mediate" position of the emotions between mind and body; or, for Spinoza in particular, between freedom and servitude, and partly due to the general ambiguity as to the meaning of emotions. To rephrase the latter statement by way of an anticipatory question: are the "emotions" something purely negative to be controlled, endured or suppressed? Or: do the so-called emotions (later to be renamed *mood*) *tell* us something about the nature of the world and ourselves and of the relation of ourselves to the world which "reason" alone cannot? In the latter case, emotions are no longer something private, subjective and psychological. They belong to the unique nature of man in that they tell him something about his manner of being in the world. (cf. Spinoza's initial statement in Part III on the emotions as being the *manner of human life*). Man and animal both share emotions or moods in some way. This is perhaps a link between them, questioning the proud assertion that man is the animal with reason; but on the other hand, the moods of the animal and man are not simply identical. One might say that man is (always) *in* a mood, whereas the animal simply *is* his mood. It is the *"in"* of his mood that distinguishes man and makes him unique.

But back to Spinoza. Instead of focusing on questions more central to a larger context, we shall concentrate on: Spinoza's fundamental distinction of active-passive, adequate and inadequate, cause and idea, reality and perfection, and *conatus* (desire, power, and the endeavor to persist in one's own being). The very *listing* of these components of Spinoza's thought is itself inadequate. We must somehow attempt to unlist these components and get at their inner relation. In doing this, we shall keep in mind the question to what extent the emotions can be called *faculties*, abilities *for* something or other, and not just hazardous jeopardizations of man's "rationality." Later on, we shall see how these faculties come to be understood and reinterpreted as manners of being in Heidegger.

The distinction active-passive is fundamental to Spinoza's thought, beginning with his definition of substance as that which is in itself and conceived through itself (i.e., active), as opposed to modes which are in another and conceived through another (passive), continuing down to his treatment of adequate and inadequate cause and idea. As a finite mode, man is inevitably "passive" to a considerable degree, subject to a multitude of external causes which affect him and over which he has no control. He is active to the limited extent that he is the adequate cause of his action and has adequate ideas of the world external to him. With respect to the emotions there is an ambiguity in this distinction of active-passive. On the one hand, Spinoza *defines* emotion as a passiveness of the soul,[6] as something which the soul *undergoes*. On the other hand, he differentiates between an emotion where we are the adequate cause of the modifications of the body and a passion where we are not.[7] But more important than this distinction between emotion and passion is Spinoza's general insight that, in spite of a proclivity to enslave human nature it is the emotions which *move* us. They take us somewhere. In this sense, they are not at all unequivocally something passive nor can it be said that we are passive to them in the sheerly limited sense that we are prey to them. In a sense which must be developed and further clarified, we *are* these emotions. There is no place and no possibility as yet in Spinoza for a kind of Freudian "unconscious" which we do not know and can "control" only with great effort.

For Spinoza, emotion is primarily a *transition*: it takes us somewhere. And where it takes us is to a greater or lesser state of perfection. Thus, built into Spinoza's very understanding of emotion is the essential fact that it can bring us to a greater state of perfection, not only to a lesser, and must thus be capable of being affirmative, and perhaps in some unique sense, active. However, Spinoza never quite relinquishes his rationalist insistence on emotion as something which can potentially enslave us and which is essentially a *confused* idea. We shall examine that aspect of his conception and return to the more positive aspect in connection with reality, perfection and power.

Spinoza attempts to eliminate a certain "value judgment," with regard to the emotions as much as possible by stating that they are as much a part of the nature of things as anything else. Although we are bound to speak of the emotions as "good" or "bad," as pleasant and positive or painful and negative, Spinoza states emphatically at the outset that they are not due to some defect of nature. There can be for him no defect in nature itself since nature is what it is, and necessarily so. Any value judgments on our part simply arise from our own lack of understanding. Negative emotions, such as hate, follow from the same necessity of nature as other individual things, and are not to be understood as something contrary to nature. Thus, Spinoza announces that he will regard human actions and desires in the same way as he treats God and the mind, as if he were dealing with the lines, planes and bodies of geometry. Human weakness and inconstancy simply follow from the ordinary power of nature and not, as Spinoza's predecessors thought, from some defect or depravity of human nature.

Spinoza's general definition of the emotions given at the conclusion of Book III is that emotion, called a passiveness of the soul, is a confused idea wherewith the mind affirms a greater or less power of existing (*vis existendi*) of its body. The key phrase in this definition is "power of existing."

The active aspect of a finite being is its endeavor (*conatus*) to persist in its own being. "Everything insofar as it is in itself endeavors to persist in its own being."[8] The "passivity" and ultimately the destruction (perhaps the ultimate form of passivity and powerlessness) to which every being is subject are not contained in the essence of the being itself, but are solely due to external causes. If the essence of a thing contained its own destruction within itself, this would be a raw contradiction.

Thus, the more adequate ideas of adequate causes a finite being has, the more active it becomes in its endeavor to persist in its own being. Its power of existing increases, bringing it to a greater degree of perfection and reality. This increase is accompanied by a feeling of pleasure (more power of existing) and brings us to a fuller participation in the divine nature. One might say that as a finite being becomes more active, powerful and perfect, it becomes more "real." One aspect of becoming more "real" lies in diminishing the characteristic of being *in another* which is the mark of the finite being. Substance is that which is in itself, the finite mode is that which is in another. But the "positive" possibilities of the finite being: becoming more active, and attaining the third kind of knowledge, intuitive science,[9] serve to diminish the "otherness" confronting the finite being. From this third kind of knowledge eventuates the intellectual love of God which is ultimately the love with which God loves himself insofar as He can be manifested through the essence of the human mind.[10]

Otherness manifests itself in two ways for Spinoza, as God who is the other in which things are and as the power of external causes to which every being is subject and which infinitely surpasses its power. The otherness of these external causes can be overcome to some extent by checking the emotions and by an understanding of the necessity in things. The otherness of God can be breached to a perhaps greater degree by the intellectual love of Him.

Although a certain ambiguity remains throughout Spinoza's attitude toward the emotions, we can in the conclusion of this discussion point out their possible "positive" function. At the end of Book Four, Spinoza states:

> But it is to be observed that when I say 'a greater or less power of existence than before,' I do not mean that the mind compares the present with the past constitution of the body, but that the idea which constitutes the reality of an emotion affirms something of the body which actually involves more or less reality than before.[11]

This is surely a difficult passage. But the general gist of it seems to hinge on the question of *reality*. What is the difference between the statements: (1) The mind compares the present condition of the body with its past condition; and (2) The idea which constitutes the form of the emotion (which is an idea expressing the disposition of the body) *affirms something* about the body whereby more or less reality (perfection) is *really* involved than before? The first statement indicates a comparison performed only by the mind which ascertains a difference between its present and past state. There is no transition to a greater or lesser *reality* of the *body* involved here. The second statement, however, does entail such a transition. Spinoza seems to be saying that, as opposed to a sheerly mental comparison of bodily states, an emotion is something which actually involves a transition from one bodily state to another one possessing more or less reality. If this transition is brought about in the direction of more reality and thus also for Spinoza, more pleasure, we come to partake of the divine nature to a greater degree and, in a sense, to overcome the "otherness" of God. "For the greater the joy with which we are affected, the greater the perfection to which we pass, and consequently the more do we participate in the divine nature."[12]

Whereas Spinoza is dealing specifically with the non-rational faculties as the emotions, primarily as the main factor in human bondage, Leibniz, the last of the strictly rationalistic thinkers to be considered here, has quite a different slant on these faculties. Leibniz is perhaps the thinker of this period who most successfully unites mind and matter, in a way not unlike Aristotle. His new interpretation of matter and mind grows out of a critical dialogue with Descartes, Spinoza and Locke, if we restrict that dialogue to the philosophers, leaving aside the equally important dialogue with the "scientists" of his time. Against the Cartesian conception of matter as extension, Leibniz argues that the essence of matter is force, thus providing a more "dynamic" understanding of matter which is potentially directed toward and striving to become mind. Against the absolute necessity of Spinoza's world of substance, Leibniz supports the free will of God and introduces the rather unique idea of inclination, being inclined as opposed to being necessitated. But these innovative conceptions are less important for our purposes than Leibniz' critical dialogue with Locke, particularly as expressed in his *New Essays on the Human Understanding*, his answer to Locke's own essay. It is a well-known fact that Leibniz objected to Locke's empiricist conception of the mind as a *tabula rasa*, a blank tablet. But not only does Leibniz argue for certain "innate" properties of the mind as against Locke; the mind is constantly *active*, even when we are unaware of this consciously. Just as for Leibniz matter is never simply static extension, mind is never inactive or empty. Leibniz is the first major thinker of his tradition to adumbrate something like a theory of the "unconscious." But Leibniz's "unconscious" has little or nothing to do with that of Freud and subsequent psychologists. The "contents" of Leibniz' "unconscious" are not material repressed because of the inability to assimilate or accept it. They never *reach* the threshold of consciousness, and yet they have a profound influence on us. More strongly than in the case of Spinoza, we are dealing in Leibniz with a kind of non-rational faculty which is not opposed to reason and which has an important, positive function.

We shall examine three concepts in Leibniz in relative isolation from the rest of his thought, insofar as that is possible, three concepts which are inextricably related to each other: minute perceptions, minute solicitations, and uneasiness or *inquiétude*, which he discusses with reference to Locke. It is our contention that these non-rational faculties still work in cooperation with reason, not against it, and that the broader view of man afforded by the inclusion of these faculties gets distorted in the subsequent *revolt* against reason and the glorification of the irrational (Chapter Three). Heidegger saw this when he stated in *Being and Time*: "When irrationalism, as the counter play of rationalism, talks about things to which rationalism is blind, it does so only with a squint."[13]

As we stated before, Leibniz maintains that, just as a substance can never be without activity, the mind is never without a myriad of perceptions, although these perceptions may not be accompanied by apperception and reflection; i.e., we may not be conscious of them in any explicit sense. Here, the problem arises of how we can speak about the unconscious, that of which we are by definition not conscious. But this problem does not pose the difficulty for Leibniz that it does for later thinkers, for his minute perceptions are, after all, minimally conscious in an unclear way. If we focus our attention upon them we can become aware that they are there. The reason that we are not ordinarily aware of them is that they are "either too slight or in too great a number or too even, so that they have nothing sufficient to distinguish them one from the other."[14] Leibniz gives the examples of the noise produced by a mill or a waterfall when we have lived near them for some time which, when they become destitute of the charms of novelty, soon fail to attract our attention. We grow accustomed to them, and are no longer "conscious" of them in the sense of paying attention to them. His other main example is that of the roar of the sea. We are not aware of the effect of each wave of the sea, and yet it must have an effect upon us, however small, since "one hundred thousand nothings cannot make something." One is reminded here of

Zeno's paradox of the millet seeds that if a tenth of a grain makes no noise when it falls, then how can a bushel consisting of these grains make a noise when it falls?

In the course of the *New Essays*, Leibniz attributes more and more significance to these minute perceptions. They explain the fact that "the present is big with the future and laden with the past," and they even constitute the identity of the individual. They "*determine* us in many a juncture without our thinking ... and they cause that *uneasiness* which I show consists in something which does not differ from pain except as the small from the great, and which nevertheless often constitutes our desire and even our pleasure, in giving to it a stimulating flavor."[15]

With this last statement, we have reached the question of the modes of pleasure and pain, and it is in the chapter of the *New Essays* entitled "Of Modes of Pleasure and Pain" that Leibniz most fully develops the concepts of uneasiness and minute solicitations. For Leibniz, pleasure and pain are not "fringe phenomena" as they had sometimes been treated by his predecessors; but, rather, a central component in every perception or experience.

"I believe that there are no perceptions which are entirely indifferent to us."[16]

In contrast to Descartes and even Spinoza, Leibniz is saying that there is no such thing as a "pure" perception unaccompanied by some affective state. Whereas his *vis* and *appetitus* which constitute the active, striving nature of things, are undoubtedly related to Spinoza's *conatus*, they go beyond that *conatus* in that they involve an accompanying affective state which has more ontological status than do the emotions in Spinoza. In a way, both conceptions herald the importance of the will in Schopenhaur, Nietzsche and German Idealism, in the latter case especially in Schelling for whom "all primal Being is will," without, however, exactly coinciding with the concept of will. However, these conceptions are at the same time both more and less than the concept of will. Less, since they do not necessarily imply the full phenomenon of conscious willing. More, because they do involve an affective state not traditionally contained in the concept of will.

Leibniz' theory of minute perceptions, absent in Locke,

leads him to accept Locke's theory of uneasiness while trans-
forming it for his own purposes. There are, obviously, two
factors in minute perceptions. First of all, they are *perceptions*,
and as such have a subliminal effect upon us, inclining us one
way or another, steering our uneasiness in one direction or
another. However, these perceptions are *minute*. We are, so to
speak, shielded from a hyper-sensitive overawareness of everything around us. Leibniz even feels that "the wise author of our
being has acted for our own good when He ordained that we
should often be in ignorance and confused perceptions."[17] Otherwise, our instincts would be stifled by oversensitivity and hunger, for instance, would be a painful experience instead of a
functional one leading to satisfaction. Leibniz's examples for
this oversensitivity are those of too keen a sense of smell, causing
discomfort, or too piercing a sense of vision which would see
all sorts of disgusting things normally hidden from us and finally,
as the epitome of these examples, he asks: "How many insects
do we not swallow without our being conscious of it?"

These minute perceptions seem to constitute the basic factor
of uneasiness in our being, although Leibniz is not very explicit
in differentiating and relating them to that uneasiness. What is
perhaps most important about the concept of uneasiness is to
see that, in spite of its linguistic form of being a "negative" or
"privative" word, its *meaning* is not negative, but rather neutral
and ultimately, for Leibniz, even quite positive.[18] He adopts the
French word *inquiétude* for the English uneasiness, stating that
if uneasiness stands for a displeasure, fretfulness (*chagrin*), discomfort or some affective pain, then it would be inappropriate
for his own conception. For Leibniz, uneasiness is not pain; but,
rather, the disposition and preparation for "pain" inherent in
desire. He states that the satisfaction of desire consists in the
victory over these semi-pains or uneasiness, yielding many semi-
pleasures which in the end become an entire and real pleasure.
Later in the same passage, Leibniz takes the final step and states
that: "Without these semi-pains there would be no pleasure and
there would be no means of perceiving that something, by being
an obstacle which prevents us from putting ourselves at our
ease, assists and aids us." Here it becomes clear that it is not
uneasiness which is a problem for human nature; but, rather,

precisely its opposite: *ease*. Without uneasiness, without the "minute imperceptible solicitations which keep us always in suspense"[19] we would stagnate and fall prey to the numbness of habit. The minute imperceptible solicitations are "like so many small springs which try to unbend, and which cause our machine to act."[20]

The "mechanistic" symbolism, often expressed in terms of the clock, quite applicable to the realm of nature and in a way spanning the two realms of nature and grace when considered with reference to God as the author of the pre-established harmony between the two realms, is also applied to the concept of uneasiness which Leibniz relates to the German term *Unruhe*, literally uneasiness, but more specifically designating the pendulum of a clock. We have, ultimately in some *non*-mechanistic way, something like a pendulum (*Unruhe*) within us, something which will not allow us to stagnate in some moribund state of ease but which is the true wellspring of our being. "As to *uneasiness*, there is in pain, and consequently in sorrow, something more; and there is uneasiness even in our joy for it makes men wide awake, active, full of hope for going further.[21]

CHAPTER 3

Irrationalism: The Revolt against Reason

The preceding two chapters attempted to sketch out something like a development in the history of reason and the difficulties posed to the supremacy of reason by the non-rational faculties. Chapter 3 on the revolt against reason and Chapter 4 on the temporalization of consciousness can no longer be said to represent a development; but, rather, two radical shifts of gear which at first glance do not seem to be directly related to each other. They are not even directly related as two revolts against the same thing since the phenomenon of the temporalization of consciousness is in no way a revolt but rather an original breakthrough into a new philosophic dimension.

Thus, we shall partially abandon our historical approach, insofar as this is possible, and simply try to analyze, for instance, under what banner "irrationalism" marches off to wage its rather blantant war on reason.

We might begin our task by asking the general question: What are the possible *alternatives* to reason and the rational, the alternatives posed by irrationalism and by other possible views of human nature which are not strictly rational? Irrationalism as instantiated by Schopenhauer, or even Freud, sees the opponent of reason as the "will," not the will of the tradition of philosophy which has always included or been intimately related to reason; but a will rather closer to "instinct," a blind driving force or Freud's *id*. What is important here is that this will or drive is more basic and more *real* than any so-called reason which is ultimately the helpless plaything of the will. Whereas the emotions discussed in Chapter 2 were not at all necessarily inimical to reason, the blind, striving will or drive is distinctly antithetical to reason and, moreover, far more fundamental. Here reason seems to be the fond, futile dream of the would-be rational animal.

In addition to the irrational which is counter to reason and the non-rational which is at first neutrally related to reason, two other alternatives would be: (1) the Buddhist conception of reality as suchness or isness, a position close to Spinoza's *amor fati* (Reality can neither be called rational nor irrational; it simply *is*. We shall return to this profound and difficult problem later.); and (2) the other alternative to the rational would be the supra- or transrational, that which is not counter to reason but transcends it and remains inaccessible to it.

Now, what about the irrational? At first there is the obvious, formal predicament of having to use reason to analyze and speak of something which runs counter to reason. We shall not take this predicament as an absolute *aporia*; but, rather, see how far the boundaries of this formal difficulty can be pushed back. To an extent one might say that we are always trying to push back the boundaries of what we can know and never succeeding except in part. Perhaps reason has limitations in a way far less "localized" than Kant conceived them—limitations ultimately restricted to the questions of the world, the soul, and God.

One of the most fundamental questions about the irrational is one which may seem at first to be no problem at all, the approximate equation of the irrational with the unconscious in the 19th century. As far as we know, the terms rational-irrational were first used by Seneca[1] who, historically speaking, could not have related the irrational to the unconscious.

In order to disentangle the maze of problems involved here, all of which it would be impossible even to touch upon in this study, let us select the following topics for discussion.

1. The relation of the irrational to the unconscious.

2. Tentatively formulated, the relation of the irrational

to the "self," a problem which we have not even mentioned up to now.

If we can succeed in gaining some clarity on these two issues
in general, we shall be ready to move on to the question of the
temporalization of consciousness.

Two questions which immediately present themselves with
regard to the relation of the irrational and the unconscious are
those of control and illusion, two seemingly disparate questions.
But only seemingly. If we take the unconscious as some kind of
blind force which is potentially destructive or at least deleterious
in some sense, the problem immediately arises of how to cope
and live with this force, especially if we cannot "know" it directly or perhaps not at all. The prototype model here is that
of an individual being of dubious ontological—or psychological—status grappling with the assaults upon him of some
stronger, utterly *alien* force. We are concerned here with the
factor of control; but when we come to the second question of
the self, the problem of the *alien* element will become acute. By
way of anticipation, let us just say that the impoverished schema
of self-other has dominated our thinking, both philosophical
and everyday, for a long time and has, in fact, so entrenched
itself that it is extremely difficult to think of anything else. To
state the problem without going into it any further at this point:
Just because something which I experience or undergo does not
come from "me" does not *eo ipso* mean that it comes from
some other, alien being or power. This is a paradoxical but not
contradictory statement, if one still worries about the rules of
logical contradiction.

But back to the question of control which, of course, does
serve to point up the element of otherness. Even when we speak
of self-control, some kind of otherness is implicitly posited in
the self in order for one element to control another.

In discussing control and then illusion we shall, of necessity,
have to remain somewhat up in the air until we can afterwards
attempt to pin down the relation of the irrational to the unconscious. In other words, we do not yet know precisely what
is controlling what or what is deceiving what. Perhaps it would
have been more advisable to start with the central question of

the relation of the irrational to the unconscious and then move on to the more concrete relations. But this method is probably too difficult for us since it involves the additional problem of the subject-object split. All of the old, stubborn cliché dichotomies get into the act at that point. However, as Spinoza would say: "Nor can I explain this more clearly at present." Since irrationalism is a rather superficial philosophic position anyhow, as we shall attempt to show, we shall choose a rather superficial philosopher in our opinion in whom the whole course of the "irrational" erupted in a strikingly clear if not unproblematic way. That philosopher is Schopenhauer. One must also note that he had an enormous influence on just about everybody at the turn of the century, not only on the academic philosophers who tended to spurn him. This influence subsequently subsided quite rapidly. Perhaps one of the main channels in which Schopenhauer remains alive for us today is through his once-devoted disciple, Nietzsche. Thus, we shall focus this chapter on discussion and critical analysis of these two thinkers since the really *philosophic* problems are set clearly in relief. Of course, we cannot deal with the irrational without some brief discussion of Freud, who will be mentioned toward the end of this chapter.

In discussing Schopenhauer and Nietzsche, let it be emphasized at the very outset that it is Schopenhauer who is the irrationalist, *not* Nietzsche, however much these two thinkers have been lumped together insofar as Schopenhauer has been considered seriously in a sustained way at all and not just read with fascination. Thus, what we want to discover is Schopenhauer's brand of irrationalism as a revolt against "reason" and what he understands by that term, and then Nietzsche's infinitely more subtle position growing out of his intense inner dialogue with Schopenhauer and his ultimate, profound rejection of him. The first thing to do is to see what kind of *problems* are at stake here.

A discussion of Schopenhauer has the additional advantage that it may provide a bridge to the fifth and final chapter on Buddhism. Since Schopenhauer is probably the first well-known philosopher in the west to incorporate eastern ideas in his thought, we get a chance to see how the very different ways of thinking in the east come into an encounter with western concepts. Of course, Schopenhauer cannot be equated with Buddhism, and as the Zen people say: "A hair's breadth makes all the difference." But, this is a pretty thick hair.

Thus, leaving the relationship of the irrational to the unconscious in the background for now we come to the question of control. Given the relation of an individual to a blind, driving force such as Schopenhauer's will or Freud's *id* or *libido*, what can that individual do about that relationship? Is he helpless in the face of that force and thus the plaything of a *general*, alien force which, uncannily, really *belongs* to no one? For the alien element in Schopenhauer's will or Freud's *id is* uncanny. I by no means intend to equate these two, but the similarities between them suffice for our purposes here. The will or *id* seems to be a free-floating force which, so to speak, at times "inhabits" or "takes over" individuals.

It is precisely on this point that Nietzsche most severely and adamantly attacks Schopenhauer. After gradually distancing himself from his initial infatuation with Schopenhauer, Nietzsche came to feel that Schopenhauer had confused the will with drive and instinct.

> *Schopenhauer's* basic misunderstanding of the *will* (as if craving, instinct, drive, were the *essence* of will) is typical: lowering the value of the will to the point of making a real mistake. Also hatred against willing; attempt to see something higher, indeed that which is higher and valuable, in willing no more, in 'being a subject *without* aim and purpose' (in the 'pure subject free of will'). Great symptom of the *exhaustion* or the *weakness* of the *will*: for the will is precisely that which treats cravings as their master and appoints to them their way and measure."[2]

Nietzsche's more mature criticisms of Schopenhauer are endless, and we only want to distill the essence of his objections to the concept of the will to live. The will to live is a senseless concept for Nietzsche who states (roughly paraphrasing) that what is alive does not need to will to live and what is not alive cannot will at all. Nietzsche's answer to Schopenhauer is his concept of the will to *power*, something quite different from the will to live. The main difference between these two thinkers is that Schopenhauer's will is essentially a blind drive whereas

Nietzsche's will essentially incorporates power and control, ultimately power over oneself and self-control.[3] The issue at stake here is whether "will" or *the* Will is a blind (unconscious) driving irrational force or whether it includes and embodies some kind of rational control and *actual* ability to exercise power-ful command over oneself. Schopenhauer's will is "irrational" for several reasons which are all interconnected. It is basically "irrational" because it "makes no sense"[4] and is engaged in an utterly futile enterprise. The two basic irrational elements in the Will are (1) that it is blind and, hence, cannot know what it is striving for; and (2) that it is intrinsically incapable of finding any satisfaction or appeasement through its willing. The nature of the Will is suffering and want, and thus it strives to gain release from itself (Schopenhauer's rather garbled understanding of "nirvana") in two ways: (1) It can try to find rest in the Will-less contemplation of art which embodies the Platonic Ideas. This attempt affords only a partial denial of the Will since it cannot be sustained. And, (2) it can attempt to deny all willing completely in the self-abnegation of the "mystic." But the Will's enterprise is doomed from the outset. If the nature of the world is Will and only Will, its striving is endless since there is nothing else in the world to countermand that striving. This Schopenhauer repeatedly makes very clear.

> The Will dispenses altogether with a final goal and aim. It always strives, for striving is its sole nature, which no attained goal can put an end to. Therefore, it is not susceptible of any final satisfaction, but can only be restrained by hindrances, while in itself it goes on forever.[5]

The Will oscillates between want (suffering) and ennui (the boredom and loss of interest in what it has attained). Thus, it is irrational in a double way. It is powerless, having no control over what it is doing, and it is without knowledge, blind and basically caught in the illusion that it might attain satisfaction and come to rest. The Will has no *control*, and it is thoroughly *deluded*. Schopenhauer's description of the Will is hardly very "aesthetic."

"For this is the Will living in both [*the thing in itself and the phenomenon, the Will and its illusory individuation in appearance*], which here, deceived by the knowledge which is bound to its service, does not recognize itself, and seeking an increased happiness in *one* of its phenomena, produces great suffering in *another*, and thus, in the pressure of excitement, buries its teeth in its own flesh, not knowing that it always injures only itself, revealing in this form, through the medium of individuality, the conflict in itself which it bears in its inner nature.[6] (Words in italics mine)

This is surely a doleful situation. Not only is Schopenhauer a proponent of irrationalism, he is a proponent of nihilism, a nihilism which has no history—as it did for Nietzsche and, later, Heidegger—but is the timeless, irremediable state of the world. The conclusion of *The World as Will and Idea* expresses this very clearly and unmasks Schopenhauer as a pseudo-mystic with little, or at best, a perverted access to the great tradition of mysticism.

"We must banish the dark impression of that nothingness which we discern behind all virtue and holiness as their final goal, and which we fear as children fear the dark; we must not even evade it like the Indians, through myths and meaningless words, such as reabsorption in Brahma or the nirvana of the Buddhists. Rather do we freely acknowledge that what remains after the entire abolition of Will is for all those who are still full of Will certainly nothing; but, conversely, to those in whom the Will has turned and denied itself, this our world, which is so real, with all its suns and milky-ways—is nothing."[7]

Either way—nothing. The Will is impotent, has no control, and it is deluded. The next final logical stage of this kind of irrationalism can be found in the conception of the world as absurd, notably in Camus and in a somewhat different way, in Beckett.[8] Camus criticizes Sartre for still believing that "freedom" is meaningful. Sisyphus keeps rolling the stone back up the hill, because there is nothing else for him to do, and he must do *something*. And Vladimir and Estragon wait, *not* FOR *Godot*; they simply wait, because, lacking the guts to kill themselves, there is, again, nothing else to do; and they must do *something*.

Let us now approach the question of the relation of the irrational and the unconscious. First of all, the unconscious is the broader concept. There are a great many of our life processes of which we are barely conscious, or not at all; for instance, the processes of the body called "involuntary," beating of the heart, function of the glands, digestion, etc. There are normally not so many elements in our behavior which could be called outspokenly irrational. Furthermore, a person who behaves irrationally may well be quite *conscious* of what he is doing. A compulsive person, for example,—and everybody is a little bit compulsive—knows quite well that he is avoiding cracks on the sidewalk or straightening up a desk which he straightened up ten minutes before. The irrationally compulsive person may be unable to say *why* he must do such-and-such a thing; but he usually knows *that* he is doing it.[9]

Granted that the concept of the unconscious is larger than that of the irrational, still we shall deal with it as it is conceived in opposition to the rational faculties. Jung's highly interesting, controversial idea of a creative "collective unconscious" docs not contain such an opposition and thus cannot directly serve the purposes of our inquiry, even though it presents a very interesting problematic in itself.

Perhaps the most important and the most *uncanny* thing about the unconscious is that it *belongs to no one*. This statement, however, must be qualified and differentiated since we are dealing with a complex and difficult phenomenon. Jung's collective unconscious does not belong to me, is not my exclusive property, precisely because it is *collective*. It can be potentially appropriated by anyone experiencing areas of his psychic development (the shadow, the wise old man, etc.), especially by the intuitive artist. The collective unconscious seems to function as a kind of "reservoir" with an individual reality of its own.

Freud's unconscious seems not to belong to me, and yet it belongs precisely to me in an insidious way which threatens my ego. According to Freud, everyone has to grapple with the unconscious in that we are all trying to cope with the same kinds of morbid, infantile repression. And yet it is *my personal* encounter with the results and blocks produced by this repression which determine my life adjustments.

This is not a psychological study of Freud. That would lie outside the scope of my competence, and would also not further the aim of this study. What I'm interested in are a few of the *philosophical* implications of Freud's work. I am assuming, perhaps erroneously, that the reader has some familiarity at least with the layman's understanding, and perhaps also with later criticism which inevitably followed such a pioneer. Thus, I am omitting a great deal of the scientific underpinnings which would be requisite for a thorough psychological study. Perhaps I may be forgiven for the broad and sweeping, but tentative, character of my statements.

Freud distinguishes between the preconscious, consisting of latent, weak ideas which can become conscious if they become stronger, and the unconscious, consisting of ideas which are intensely active but do not normally enter consciousness.[10] It is the latter, the unconscious, with which Freud is primarily concerned. What is unconscious in us strongly resists being known, and yet it ought to be known for the sake of the psychic health of the individual to the extent that he is capable of assimilating what is unconscious. In his very subtle essay on the uncanny (*das Unheimliche*[11]), Freud suggests that the very power of the uncanny rests in the fact that it is dimly, threateningly familiar as in, for example, the case of the phantom double (*Doppelgaenger*).

To try to disentangle this somewhat chaotic plethora of remarks, let us try to summarize in what sense the unconscious of Freud belongs, or does not belong, to me, in what sense it is related, or relatable, to my ego, or is alien to that ego. The unconscious does not belong to me, in the sense that I am unaware of it, and unrelated consciously to it. In that sense, it represents an alien force potentially threatening to overpower the ego and its defenses which, however, according to Freud, can never be fully overpowered. In another sense, the unconscious, whose contents are fundamentally *structurally* the same for everybody[12] is related to the individual in a very *personal* way as far as *content*. Thus, the unconscious is neither mine nor not-mine, and this gives it its ominous force.

One of Freud's most important tenets is that the unconscious is, by far, what is most *"real"* in the pragmatic sense of that term. It is most real precisely because it is neither mine nor not-mine. I can never really know it, assimilate it, and appropriate it; nor can I ignore it and dispense with it. All I can do is to try to live with and live out my situation. I am at the mercy of something which is inseparable from me, and yet is not "me."

Who is this "me"? This brings us to the question of the self and its relation to the unconscious. For Freud, the self is the ego, the "general narcissism of mankind" which has received three deadly blows from the "researches of science."[13] These blows are cosmological (Copernicus' discovery that the earth is not the center of the universe), biological (Darwin's assertion that man is not essentially different from the animal, nor superior to him), and, worst of all, psychological. The psychological blow is to be found in Freud's own research culminating in the statement that *"the ego is not master in its own house."*[14] "The life of the sexual instincts cannot be totally restrained, and mental processes are in themselves unconscious and only reach the ego and come under its control through incomplete and untrustworthy perceptions."[15]

But the question is: Is what Freud calls the ego, together with its ultimately futile and insoluble relation to the unconscious, is this ego *what or who we really are?*

Who are we? What is the self? This is perhaps *the* supreme philosophical question. For, as Leibniz pointed out in his *Monadology*,[16] if we could know *completely* any one "body" (or self), which is, of course, not possible, we would know the whole universe together with its entire past and future.

The spectrum of answers to this question is broad, ranging from the one extreme of "behaviorism" (the self is a behavioristically determined string of events with no core or separate reality apart from the sense impressions of these events) to the other extreme of a transcendental, substantial—usually, in some sense, "immortal"—"entity." In all of these approaches, however divergent, the problem of the relation of the various faculties—senses, will, emotions, reason—to the so-called "self" remains obscure. Is the self something which "has" these faculties? Is it their unifying principle? Is the self the "subjective" counterpart to the "substantiality" of the object? For both terms, subject and substance have the same basic etymological meaning: to stand or throw under, to underlie and persist through change. In most analyses of "personal identity," this underlying of the self boils down to the factor of memory. It is chiefly ' memory which gives us our sense of the continuity of self.

A new direction to these questions about the self—not an outright "answer"—will be taken in the next chapter dealing with the temporalization of consciousness. Simply expressed, when the self is conceived as a *process* and not as substance or subject, the problem takes on a different aspect. We are asked to think a new kind of "unity" of the self.

A distinction has been frequently, if not consistently, drawn between the ego and the Self. Broadly and generally speaking, this distinction often conceives the ego as something more than Freud's localization of defense mechanisms, yet it is still a relatively narrow and "egotistical" sphere of the individual as opposed to the Self which is a more fundamental and all-encompassing sphere of that individual. I use the word all-encompassing because I somehow wish to avoid the word "universal" for reasons which will become clear later. The most important thing about the latter concept of Self is that the Self *is* the most fundamental level of reality and, thus, does not stand in opposition to the unconscious. In fact, the unconscious plays little or no role whatsoever in this concept of the Self. Most of the so-called existential psychiatrists, for example, dispense with the unconscious since they feel that such a concept contains too many imponderable, completely unverifiable assumptions and also does not facilitate an understanding of the individual in the world. This rejection of the unconscious is, at the same time, more scientific and pragmatic. As Rollo May says

Perhaps the most handy anxiety-reducing agent is to abstract one's self from the issues by assuming a wholly-technical emphasis. These men (existential psychotherapists) resisted this temptation. They, likewise, were unwilling to postulate unverifiable agents, such as 'libido,' or 'censor,' . . . or the various processes lumped under "transference" to explain what was going on. And they had particularly strong doubts about using the theory of the unconscious as a *carte blanche* on which almost any explanation could be written. They were aware, as

Straus puts it, that the 'unconscious ideas of the patient are more often than not the conscious theories of the therapist.' [17]

Instead of attempting to reduce anxiety (Freud's aim), the existential psychiatrists accept it, not only as something which *absolutely belongs* to man's nature, but as something the experience of which is *essential* to becoming a full human being instead of getting dispersed in banalities and drowning in trivia. Thus, Laing writes of "ontological insecurity," an insecurity which is not merely psychological but potentially rooted in human nature itself.

This new relation to *angst* derives, of course, from Heidegger who had a profound influence on existential psychiatry, the "science" upon which he had the most direct and overwhelming effect. The term, *angst*, originating with Kierkegaard, has no precise equivalent in English. "Anxiety," in spite of its etymological root of meaning "hemmed in" (*angustiae*, the narrows), has too many connotations of being anxious or even nervous *about* something, whereas the impact of *angst* lies precisely in the fact that it is *angst* about nothing, no thing in particular. The same difficulty applies to the term dread. We say: I dread Monday mornings, something all too specific.

If we are not dealing with a pathologically disturbed person—and that lies outside the scope and concern of this inquiry—the experience of *angst* is fundamental to man; it brings him face-to-face with his own finitude. The psycho-*analytic* attempt to get rid of or reduce it is the psychological counterpart to the Cartesian epistemological ideal of *certainty*. We want *security*, at any cost. Security is more desirable than "authenticity."

It is a basic insight of existential psychiatry that, once you divide the human being into subject-object, mind-body, ego-superego-id, heredity-environment, you will never get these factors thus divided back together again in any genuine way. Once you do this, you are simply going to run out of hyphens (psychosomatic, etc.). The point of departure must be being-in-the-world. There is no such thing as a worldless self to be investigated. The self is always in the world and never to be found without it. The worldless self, for example, of Husserl's philosophy, is an abstraction.

One very central point follows from all this: The fact that there are things which I cannot *know* and cannot *control* by no means leads to the conclusion that these things are more *real* than what I can know and control. The fact that something is unconscious or not completely conscious does not vouch for its more powerful reality at all. It might simply be *irrelevant*. How many "thoughts" come into our mind every day of our lives which have little or nothing to do with us? These thoughts may appear frightening if we take them seriously. I might think: Well, I could kill my mother-in-law. The fact is, I don't want to kill my mother-in-law at all; this is just one more possible ghost of a thought running through my head as I sit, for instance, bored and somewhat stultified on a subway on the way to work. Most of us do not reach the point of Gide's character who pushed the man out of the train "for no reason." These ghost thoughts do not lead anywhere. They are unrelated to us, they belong to no one, they are trivial and silly.

Any one who has ever tried to "meditate" or to even sit down and think of "nothing," must have experienced this phenomenon. Try to think of nothing in particular, and every possible and impossible thought races into your head.

But enough of this. The point being made here in a rather long-winded way is that the strangeness of thoughts says nothing about their status of being more real. It might be far more important, for example, that I remember that I must lock the door when I leave the house.

To conclude this chapter and to lead into the following ones, two final remarks with regard to the unconscious should be made. The first touches upon what Buddhism has to say about the unconscious (Chapter 5). The second should lead us into what Heidegger has to say about the self in general before going into his understanding of the temporality of that self (*consciousness* in our general language, *Da-sein* in his). With regard to the first remark, I only want to point out Suzuki's comparison of the unconscious of psychoanalysis with that of Buddhism. To go into this question in any depth would require another book, a book which I do not intend to write.

In his book, *The Zen Doctrine of No-Mind*, Suzuki states:

> The unconscious reflects on its surface all such thought-instants, which pass with the utmost rapidity while it itself remains serene and undisturbed. These passing thoughts constitute my consciousness, and insofar as the latter is regarded as belonging to me, it has no connection with the unconscious, and there are attachments, hankerings, worries, disappointments, and all kinds of 'evil thereof.' When they are, however, connected with the unconscious, they fall away from my consciousness; they cease to be evils, and I share the serenity of the unconscious. . . .
>
> The conception of the unconscious leads to many wrong interpretations when it is taken as pointing to the existence of an entity to be designated 'the unconscious.'[18]

This conception of the unconscious is not that of an unknown entity lying "beneath" my ego. The unconscious is rather self-nature, the true Buddha-nature in everyone of which we are initially unaware.

It is a strange phenomenon that in the eighteenth and nineteenth centuries there are two diametrically opposed interpretations of the meaning of "consciousness." One is the idea that all nature culminates in man, in his consciousness (Goethe, German Idealism). Nature becomes, so to speak, aware of itself in man. The other idea is that it is precisely man's consciousness in the sense of self-consciousness which interferes with his functioning, blocks him, hinders him (Nietzsche, Kleist's Marionette Theatre). The Buddhist position is remarkably close to the second interpretation.

> Some may say that physical goods are not the same as psychological functions, that without the latter there is no mind and without a mind no sentient being. But I say, without these physical possessions which you are supposed to be in need of, where is your body? Without the body, where's the mind? After all, these psychological functions do not belong to you to the same extent as your clothes, your table, your family, your body, etc., belong to you. You are always controlled by them, instead of your controlling them. You are not master, even of your own body which seems to be most intimate to you. You are

subject to birth and death. With the body, your mind is most closely connected, and this seems to be still more out of your control. Are you not throughout your life a mere plaything of all your sensations, emotions, imaginations, ambitions, passions, etc.?[19]

Far from being conceived as an ego battling against its instincts, the Self in question here not only cannot be equated with its emotions, imaginations and passions, it cannot even be equated with its *thoughts*. We take leave of Descartes.

Finally, Suzuki gives a diagram[20] of *six* levels of Mind, the fundamental level in this diagrammatic spatialization being self-nature. The unconscious of psychoanalysis is the second most "superficial" level, right beneath the empirical mind.

This brief discussion leaves many loose threads hanging which we will try to pick up in Chapter 5.

We turn to Heidegger by way of transition. It is one of the most central, lasting insights of all of Heidegger's thought that we do not know what or who man is. It is most explicitly developed in *Being and Time*. Heidegger asks about the Who of *Da-sein*, of human being. But the fact that we do not know this who has nothing to do with any theory of the unconscious, a term utterly lacking in Heidegger. Neither, however, does Heidegger have anything like the self-nature of the Buddhist. Apparently, he does not have nor wish to have the experiential basis for this kind of "phenomenon." Rather, to put it simply, Heidegger's concern is to inquire how this thing we call consciousness *comes about*, with the ultimate aim of getting at the meaning of Being. I hope I may be forgiven for introducing a term such as consciousness so foreign to Heidegger, but I do want to speak as far as possible in the English language.

With the question of how consciousness comes about, we have reached the question of the temporalization of consciousness.

CHAPTER 4

The Temporalization of Consciousness

It is time to return to the initial question of this study, the question: What is real? We saw that the predominant answer in the western tradition to this question lay in the domain of reason. Reason is the key to reality. When I know *why* something is or has happened, I understand its reality.

When the seventeenth century rationalists began analyzing the role of the non-rational faculties in relation to reason, they discovered in part and within certain limitations that these faculties also constituted the nature and reality of man. The non-rational faculties hardly furnished man with the reason why, yet they could serve to heighten or diminish his *sense* of reality.

The revolt against rationalism went far beyond the rationalist's acceptance of the non-rational as constitutive of reality. What is real for these thinkers is precisely something alien and inimical to reason, forces which are far more powerful than anything rational, and thus ominous and threatening to it.

What effect does the temporalization of consciousness have upon the role of reason? What difference does it make if the human experience of reality is conceived as a *process*, and not in terms of static faculties of the mind or an unknowable entity such as the unconscious?

This is a difficult question. The element of "dynamism" was already prefigured in the revolt against rationalism. The unconscious *does* things to us. Yet this dynamic element was still conceived as an *interaction* between relatively stable and static entities such as the ego, superego, id or the will and the individual.

An analysis of temporalization or temporality strives to show, not explain, how reality *comes about*, how it *occurs*. This is the gist of Heidegger's use of the phenomenological method, to describe being-in-the-world with the preliminary aim of then showing what makes this being-in-the-world possible. This is still a far cry from analyzing *why* being-in-the-world comes about. "There is" such a thing as being-in-the-world, it is "*given.*" Heidegger's principal question in *Being and Time*, then, is: What is the *meaning* of being-in-the-world, a question which then leads him to ask how it is possible.

We must ask again: Has not the whole question of what is real shifted to the realm of subjectivity, has not everything been narrowed down to the "human mind?" What about the objective world?

Anyone who has read some Kant knows that he is not supposed to ask that kind of question anymore since all that we know of reality is, after all, our experience of it. We cannot know things as they are in themselves without our knowing them. And yet we all, even the most philosophically sophisticated of us, still have vestiges of that question in us; it seems to have permanently infiltrated our everyday lives.

Apart from the fact which we mentioned earlier that Heidegger conceives man as being-in-the-world, as a being *always in* a world and *never* without it, we should constantly keep in mind his everpresent statement that we do not know what or who man is. Thus, to say that an analysis of "consciousness" lands us in subjectivity or, for Heidegger, in psychologism, is simply to overleap the whole question of what is happening in this consciousness, let alone the question of *to whom* it belongs. We seem to take the terms subjective and psychological for granted; we all know what they mean. But this is to miss the profoundly *uncanny* experience of being aware. What I'm trying to say here is extremely difficult to express because we are so close to this awareness; in fact, we *are* it. This is probably why Heidegger chooses to discuss such a relatively unusual experience as *angst* since there is in *angst* precisely no object whatsoever to fix upon; we suddenly become aware of the uncanniness of our own consciousness. The uncanniness and also the wonder of this experience could lead us to reformulate the question: "Why is there anything at all rather than nothing?" as: How do I experience anything at all rather than nothing? Which amounts to the question: How is it that I *am* (in the world)? We take a look at things around us, tables, chairs, books, etc.; they are not aware. As Heidegger says, the chair cannot *touch* the wall, even if it is smack up against it, in the way that I can touch it. We look at trees, plants, flowers, etc.. They are not aware either, although they are alive, sentient, or sensitive to a degree. We look at animals, but already we are not just looking at them, we are interacting with them. They are aware, but in a way often inscrutable to us, because they cannot "mediate" their experience to us in language. Who has not looked at a cat, sitting quiet and motionless, as if it were thinking the most profound thought which, of course, it is not. What is going on in that cat's head? We don't know.

And then we look at man, who is aware and who often mediates far too much of what is going on in his head. Facetiousness aside, the minute we get out of the domain of everyday, perfunctory human behavior, which happens seldom enough, we are face to face with a mystery. This can happen in *angst* or other root-shaking moods, in looking at a painting, or listening to a poem or music, in rare encounters with our fellow men. We shall see that for Heidegger it is primarily *moods*, not the non-rational faculties and certainly not the irrational, which bring us before this mystery and allow us to experience "things" which are not things at all. As Heidegger says: "Irrationalism, as the counterpart of rationalism, talks about the things to which rationalism is blind, only with a squint."[1]

To return to our question: What effect does the temporalization of consciousness have upon the role of reason? We have already partially answered this question by saying that Heidegger is concerned with the process of awareness, how it comes about. He has relinquished the term reason and given us a different "break-down" of consciousness; namely, understanding, attunement, and speech. These are the three "existentials," i.e., ways in which *Da-sein is* its "there," there in the non-spatial sense of disclosedness, as when we say "he's all there," or "he's not all there." To say that *Da-sein is* its "there" is to say that *Da-sein* per-dures the there of openness. But perhaps that statement is only more obscure than the first.

Da-sein is its "there." This is the meaning of the term *ek-stasis*, also ek-sistence, to stand outside oneself and at the same time to stand within (per-dure, Instaendigkeit) that standing out. This is what temporality "is." Temporality is the original and primordial standing outside itself.

Thus, we must shift our question of the effect of the temporalization of consciousness on the role of reason to the question: What is temporality?

The question of temporality, and, on another level, the whole preoccupation of this century and the last, with time and process, is not simply on the scent of a delectable dynamism and exalting creative process.[2] It is attempting to get at the root of *presence*, better yet *presencing*, not in the sense of the extendedness in space of objects (*Vorhandenheit*), but in the sense of awareness.

The English word awareness is a valuable one. It lacks any connotation of dualism, the subject-object split, the mind-body split. Astonishingly enough, it's etymological root is the same as the German *wahr*, true, which by sheer accident—or perhaps not—links it to Heidegger's concern with truth. It has other ramifications in English, for example, in the related term wary. Wariness is a certain frame of mind or mood which knows, which is "on the lookout" for everything around it.

Temporality is the original outside itself. What does this mean? We said that Heidegger's analysis of the temporality of being-in-the-world attempts to get at the root of presencing or awareness. We are scratching at the tenuous but tenacious boundaries of language here. Heidegger's analysis almost boils down to a matter of "prepositions," to the Between of things.

This idea of Between is a basic leitmotif of all of Heidegger's thought. It can already be found in *Being and Time*.

But in that case, what else is presented with this phenomenon than the objectively-present *commercium between* an objectively present subject and an objectively present object? This interpretation would come closer to the phenomenal content if it said: *Da-sein is the being* of this 'Between.'[3]

The two main prepositions which Heidegger makes thematic for an understanding of this Between are "out" and "in," standing outside of oneself (*Aussersichstehen, ek-stasis, ek-sistence* and standing within (*Instaendigkeit, Austrag,* per-durance). Here again we are faced with the almost insurmountable difficulty which Bergson already pointed out. Our consciousness, by nature, "spatializes" things. We cannot imagine or picture anything except as objectified in space. Thus, it is not sufficient to picture this Between as, for example, the "empty" space between the walls of a chasm or the "empty" space between me and the door. Nor is it sufficient to picture the "in" as the spatial containedness of a pencil in the drawer or of the object in the room. Nor is it sufficient to picture the out—already more difficult to picture—as going out the door, as outside the house. We are asked, so to speak, to "perform" or bring about the movements of out and in within and *as* the structure of our own awareness. The only analogy, perhaps not a very good one, to this that I can think of, would be the "meditator," or whatever you want to call him, who "perceives" the arising and disappearing of his thoughts, together with whatever it is in him that allows these thoughts to arise and disappear, which itself does not arise and disappear at all. Our meditator is not "concentrating" on the thoughts themselves nor even on the conditions of the possibility of thought in general (Kant), but on the arising and disappearing together with the background of that arising and disappearing. The arising and disappearing might be compared to the out, the going outside of oneself, and the in might be compared to the "background," the holding-together of arising and disappearing while holding out (*aushalten*), per-during the Between of arising and disappearing and "Background." Already our "logic" breaks down here since logically the Background cannot be both one side of the Between and also the whole relation of Background and arising and disappearing. But no matter. Language, let alone logic, can be clumsy. One has to "*do*" this relation, not just attempt to describe it in a manner acceptable to our habitual, "logical" thinking.

Let us now see how temporality as the original Outside-Itself makes possible the three ways of being-in-the-world. Temporality is the *structural* possibility of these three ex-istentials or ways of being the "there." In other words, if I found myself in a certain mood and with a certain understanding of a situation, temporality would provide the answer with regard to how this *came about*, what made it possible, not *why* it is so. Heidegger stresses the fact that these three "ways" are equiprimordial, they always occur together and all at once and are separable only for purposes of analysis. Thus, I am never in a mood without some understanding of that mood, and I never understand something without being in a mood which "attunes" or colors my understanding. I am never without mood *and* understanding, they are always constitutive for my very being-in-the-world. Even "being indifferent" or "not understanding" are modes of mood and understanding. Heidegger characterizes them as "deficient modes," using a very effective technique enabling him to answer many possible objections. Only a being capable of mood can be indifferent. A tree is not indifferent.

The question of speech is less obviously constitutive of our being-in-the-world than the first two modes. But what Heidegger means by speech is not verbal utterance, but an inner articulation of our thoughts and feelings which may or may not become verbal. There are, after all, many things in our lives about which we are hesitant to speak, yet "speech" is constitutive for the inner articulation of those things to ourselves.

Since our aim is not an exposition of *Being and Time* as such—that would be an enormous undertaking far beyond the scope of this study, an undertaking which, furthermore, has been and is being carried out by many highly-qualified scholars—we shall try to extricate what is essential to our inquiry into the relation of temporality and reality from the intricate analyses of that book. This means, among other things, that we abstract as far as possible from the problematic of authenticity and inauthenticity which runs through all of the analyses and constitutes one of the real difficulties of the book, *Being and Time*. In Heidegger's later thought, this problematic is no longer thematic, and recedes in favor of the more "ontological" question of Appropriation and Framing or the essence of technology.

In other words, the inauthenticity of everydayness comes to correspond to man's ominous immersion in the essence of technology which is itself nothing technological at all; but, rather, the present "epoch" of Being, our present relation to Being which is *in-appropriate*. The authenticity of the self, on the other hand, comes to correspond to Appropriation, the belonging-together of man and Being envisaged if we take the step-back out of metaphysics (here conceived as the history of the oblivion of Being, nihilism, culminating in Framing, the *confrontation* of man and Being.)[4] In spite of the obvious differences in the *level* of analysis, the problem is basically the same: Authenticity (*auto*-self) and Appropriation (*proper*-self) as the possible "*genuine*" mode of relatedness.

I must apologize here for "sitting on different rungs of my ladder." (Nietzsche) I realize that some of what I am trying to say is fairly intelligible, and some of it creeps into an esoteric dimension of Heidegger's thought not so intelligible to a non-specialized thinker. But in a way, this reflects my own relation to Heidegger's thought, and thus I can scarcely avoid it.

How does temporality make being-in-the-world possible? Consistent with the emphasis on the future as the primary mode of temporality, Heidegger describes *Da-sein*'s pro-ject (*Entwurf*), its projecting itself into the future, its constant being-ahead-of-itself. In the being-ahead-of-itself of *Da-sein*, the future[5] comes toward it, and it is brought back to its already-having-been, its "past" (*Gewesenheit*), facticity and thrownness. This means that I always find myself (*befinde mich*, mood) as already having-been. I have no absolute beginning which I can ascertain. I did not make a conscious choice to be born, to exist; I simply find myself as always already having-been-thrown into the world (*Geworfenheit*).

From the "coalescence" of future and past, the present is engendered, a mode of presence incorporating future and past. Thus, the "occurrence" of "consciousness" results from the structures of temporality which makes possible being-in-the-world; existence, facticity and ensnarement in their unity, ultimately the openness to being occurring as the Opening (*Lichtung*) of being itself.

Here we must insert some remarks on the term "ensnarement." Heidegger speaks of the unity of existence, facticity and ensnarement, which could present a problem, a problem again resulting from the problematic of Authenticity and Inauthenticity. We are *always* existent and *always* factically there, as long as we are. We are *mostly*, but not *always*, ensnared in the world. Yet this factor of ensnarement particularly filters into the analyses of temporality, more so than the other phenomena of Inauthenticity, such as curiosity, idle talk, ambiguity, etc. This fact reflects Heidegger's preoccupation in the book, *Being and Time*, with the phenomenon of world which initially and, for the most part, involves getting ensnared in the things of the world as opposed to taking the resolute stand of the authentic Self. The word, *Verfallen*, which I have translated as ensnarement, has been translated as fallen, as falling into the world. Thus, there seems to be a conflict here between falling, which involves motion, and ensnarement, which does not. There is something correct about the term falling, since there is movement involved here. But it is a peculiar kind of movement. If I continually fall into a trap, as *Da-sein* continually falls toward the world, I *am ensnared*. *Verfallen* means a kind of movement *that doesn't go anywhere*; it can't. If, for instance, I *fall prey* to the charms of someone (*ich bin ihm verfallen*), I am caught, hypnotized, paralyzed; and all the movements, attempts, to get out of this state, will get me nowhere, but will rather entrench my plight.

Wherein lies the originality and significance of Heidegger's concept of temporality? What has temporality to do with our question about reality? The answers to these questions will lead us to the final consideration of this chapter—a consideration of mood, something which we briefly mentioned in Chapter 2 on the non-rational faculties.

Now, what is *"new"* about Heidegger's concept of temporality? Someone who browses long enough in the tenebrous fields of philosophy may eventually come to realize that there are *not that many new philosophical ideas*; in fact, not that many philosophical ideas at all. Heidegger himself, in his writings on the history of philosophy or metaphysics, was accustomed to say that each thinker has *one* thought, the thought ruling and guiding all of his thinking. Thus, he could succinctly discuss the history of philosophy with the help of a handfull of concepts: The One, the Logos, *idea, ousia, energeia,* substance, actuality, perception, the monad, objectivity, the being posited, or self-positing in the sense of the will of reason, love, spirit, power, the will to will in the eternal recurrence of the same. These twelve concepts take him from Plato to Nietzsche. For our purposes here, it does not matter whether Heidegger's analysis of the history of philosophy is "accurate" or arbitrary. We merely wished to illustrate the point that philosophical ideas are few and far between, and to suggest the claim that temporality is one of these ideas. Of course, temporality is not Heidegger's central interest. That is Being. Still, it was temporality that got Heidegger on the path to Being and took him as far as he was able to go. And the pervading affinity between the original Outside-Itself of temporality and the later ideas, prefigured in *Being and Time,* of Opening (*Lichtung*) and Appropriation (*Ereignis*), are unmistakable. The whole meaning of *ek-stasis,* ecstasy, existence, standing outside oneself, and the somewhat later emphasis of standing-within (man is the stand-in for nothingness, *der Platzhalter des Nichts*)[6] culminate in the late ideas of Opening, perdurance and Appropriation. One might say that *Lichtung* (Opening) is the "*there*" of Being itself, *Austrag* (perdurance) is man's reception and shepherding of that *Lichtung,* and *Ereignis* is the belonging-together of both. This characterization is probably not exactly "false," but it is, of course, misleading. But we have to go off the track sometime, if only to rest our philosophical feet. Even *Holzwege* have side trails.

These remarks are not intended simply to transpose what Heidegger means by temporality to the dimension of Being. They should only serve to point out the affinity.

What seems to me to be new about Heidegger's analysis of temporality is that it makes the almost impossible attempt to state in words what temporality is, and that means, specifically for time, *how it occurs.* Philosophers have talked about time since Heraclitus and Parmenides. Nineteenth and Twentieth Century thinkers have put an enormous emphasis on time and process, without trying or without being able to say how it occurs. The arch example for this is Hegel, whose whole philosophy rests on process, and who yet is unable to think the commensurability of dialectic and time. The dialectical process proceeds "in time" while overcoming time as something external to it. But how does this dialectical process proceed? To say that it "moves" from thesis to antithesis to synthesis or from the in-itself to the for-itself to the in-and-for-itself is not to explain or even describe that movement itself. How do we get from thesis to antithesis? By negation. By a negation which supersedes (*hebt auf*, negates) the thing in its mere individuality, preserves it in its essential being, and elevates it to a higher reality). But Hegel's concept of negation, which is positionally (positing, thetic) dialectical, is not temporal and does not really explain how the process can move.

In his discussion of time, another philosopher of a quite different ilk, Bergson, at one point states that

> There is no doubt but that for us time is at first identical with the continuity of our inner life. What is this continuity? That of a flow or passage, but a self sufficient flow or passage, the flow not implying a thing that flows, and the passage not presupposing states through which we pass; the *thing* and the *state* are only artifically taken snapshots of the transition; and this transition, all that is naturally experienced, is duration itself.[7]

This admittedly rather isolated passage from Bergson clearly shows a certain kinship with Heidegger in that it understands things and states as artificial abstractions. But when we look for what it is that is not thing or state, we are presented with terms such as continuity, flow, passage, transition, and, finally, duration. These terms all presuppose that we know *how* they flow, transit, endure; in short, *occur*. They do not describe the *structure* of occurrence. I apologize for leaning so heavily on the word structure; but it is indispensible to point toward what I am trying to get at here.

Now, *temporality* for Heidegger is not, strictly speaking, a process. It is *a structure of occurrence*. The word structure here means precisely that temporality is not something which takes place "in time," but, to use Heidegger's words, something which temporalizes itself. A "process"—the term is vague enough—

presupposes the seriality of time, its character of succession. It is precisely this seriality which Heidegger claims is a derivative conception of time going back to Aristotle's analysis of time as a series of now-points.

This is not, of course, tantamount to denying that there is process in the world. That would be ridiculous. But the structure of temporality—and on the final level of Heidegger's thought, the meaning of Being itself—is the presupposition for the nature of any possible process and is "responsible" for it. At the final level of Heidegger's thought, the destinings (*Geschicke*—literally, what is sent) and epochs of being are, so to speak, in the vernacular, a "one-shot" deal. Once an epoch of being has been sent, there remains only for the nature of that epoch to work itself out.

To be unpardonably ontic, it is as if being were the pitcher in a baseball game, throwing balls to the batter (man), who misses (nothing really happens) or hits (is appropriated to the ball). *Then* begins the process character of the epoch (strike) thus determined—the *game* as such with the outfield running around, throwing, catching, sliding, etc. The only question here is: Who is the Umpire?

I've gone about as far as I can go in indicating what is original about Heidegger's conception of temporality. It remains now to inquire into the relation of temporality and reality, which leads us to mood.

If the answer to the fundamental, pervasive, philosophical question: What is real? does not lie in giving a reason why something is and if it does not give up its character as question and land in the pragmatically successful or unsuccessful attempt to cope with that "What is real?" as something unknown and barely controllable (the unconscious as what is real), where are we now? We were hoping that a consideration of temporality would give us some new insight into what is real.

It can. But we must constantly bear in mind the fact that temporality by no means coincides with what we are accustomed to think of as time, although it is possible to derive that familiar idea of time from temporality, a separate issue in itself. Thus, even when Heidegger primarily relates understanding to the future, *attunement* to the past, and speech or articulation and

ensnarement to the present, past, present and future are not to
be thought within the framework of serial time, successive now-
points. Understanding projects toward a possibility of being for
the sake of which *Da-sein* exists. Attunement comes face-to-
face with thrownness; it finds itself as always already having
been. Thus, the structure of *Da-sein* or being-in-the-world is,
expressed as nakedly as possible, in terms of pure prepositions:
Ahead-of-itself—already-in—being-together-with. This is the
unity of existence, facticity and ensnarement, the Outside-Itself.
But being-ahead-of-itself is not "out there" in the future. It is
what enables *Da-sein* to come toward itself instead of being
dispersed and trapped in the things and events of its world. And
being already in is not "back there" in the past. It is what enables
Da-sein to come back *to* "something" instead of oscillating in
a rigidified rootlessness. Both of these, coming toward oneself
and always already finding oneself in, occur as, constitute the
fullness of the present.

Thus, a consideration of temporality can give us some insight into what is real by showing, not how we experience an
objectified present, but how our awareness comes about in terms
of understanding and attunement. Only because I am outside
myself and can come toward myself can I be *in* the world, in a
mood. The "Out" makes possible the "In," either inauthenti-
cally as being ensnared in the world or authentically as standing-
within and dwelling.

Keeping in mind the fact that it is the Outside-Itself and
coming toward itself which brings us back to the already *in* and
thus acknowledging the primacy of the future in Heidegger, I
should like to focus on this very "already being in," on attunement which is perhaps the most innovative factor in his analysis
of being-in-the-world. It is primarily mood which discloses to
me *how* I am in the world.

Attunement or mood *is* how I find myself in the world and
this *is* what is real. Mood—etymologically related to mode, the
how—is not something to be controlled and is not a confused
idea. Mood does not search back behind what is going on to
find out why it is going on. It simply is the how of the naked
that, of existence. I do not ask why am I in this mood—although
we often do that, particularly when we are in a "bad" mood—

but, rather, what is this mood, what is going on here, what does it *tell me* about myself in the world. For mood tells me things about myself in the world which just looking at things or analyzing them can never do. It simply obviates the dichotomy between reason and emotion, between my rational understanding of what occurs and my emotional re-action to it. Mood can in no way be conceived as a faculty. True, Heidegger analyzes mood in *Being and Time* in terms of how it makes being in the world possible. But we might "update" him a little to the dimension of his later thought which relinquishes the Kantian question of how something is possible—still not at all the same as asking for a reason why—and focuses on the sheer occurrence of mood.

Heidegger himself once spontaneously pointed out that what corresponds to attunement in his later writings is dwelling. Mood, attunement,[8] how we find outselves, becomes our *mode* of dwelling.[9]

But, it might be objected, apart from the fact that moods are totally subjective—the most subjective things of all, even more so than emotions which usually have a cause—are moods simply not derivative accompaniments of physiological conditions? There are two objections here, one relative to the subjective, the other to the physiological. Let us deal with the latter objection first, since we have already attempted to discuss the former which, however, is the most pervasive and stubborn of all.

The problem of physiology boils down to something like the simple question which probably everyone has asked himself at one time or another: Did I get a bad cold because I was "down" and depressed, or am I down and depressed because I have a bad cold? Here, again, it seems to be our nature to ask why something is the case, particularly when this something is negative. Actually, most people can cope better with a negative frame of mind if they know what caused it and, perhaps, know how long it will last. This is the terrible thing about pathological states of depression. There seems to be no known cause and no way of telling when they come and how long they will last.

There is, however, no end to this kind of questioning. I might want to say that I am depressed because of a bad cold.

But this explanation does not tell me *how* the cold causes me to be depressed; it only *describes* my physiological state which is the most any physiological "explanation" can do. It tells me *that* something is so, not *why*. And then I am forced to question further. Why did I get the bad cold? Possibly because I slept badly and was tired. But, then, why did I sleep badly? Something I ate? Something on my mind? We are shunted back and forth from the physical to the psychological in a way we know to be inadequate to the situation, and yet we continue to be caught in the obviously false "parallelism" of these realms of our being.

The supposed supremacy of our reason is quite jeopardized by the inexorability and the inaccessible persistence of mood. I have no *reason* to be in a bad mood, I have every reason to be content and happy. Conversely, a person quite ill or suffering from bad circumstances often sails through the day, tackling all sorts of hurdles, and remains simply untouched by them. The mood a person is in seems to determine how he meets whatever happens to him. Even if it literally has no effect on what is happening to him, it has an influence on what gets through to him.

We have seen that this kind of questioning is unfruitful. Once mind and body are conceived as separable, all we can do is go back and forth between them on the same level of attempted causal explanation. And it is not much better to assert that they are the "same," for this is practically meaningless in terms of concrete understanding. We land in inscrutability, give up the question, and go on existing.

We return to the problem of the alleged subjectivity of mood. Reason is what is objectively valid, a rational person is a stable, sensible person. Moods are totally subjective and unstable. A "moody" person is unstable, unpredictable and incomprehensible.

This view is undoubtedly correct, but it confuses mood with a kind of volatility of emotional reactions, a familiar and incontestable phenomenon which we could describe as an "ontic" consequence of mood. Only because I am "*in*" a certain mood can I react *with* certain emotions. If I am, for instance, in a mood of joy, it is hardly possible for me to react with anger at someone, no matter what he does.

The phenomena of mood, attunement, stance toward life, and attitude, are fundamentally constitutive for our being-in-the-world. They are not epiphenomena "accompanying" our experience and "coloring" it in some inessential, inexplicable way. They bring us face-to-face with "reality" if reality is not conceived as the objective presence (*Vorhandenheit*) of a world which is an abstraction and belongs to no one. Just because the experience of reality has to belong to someone does not mean it is, therefore, subjective, especially if we are unable to define human being as a subject. Temporality is centrally instrumental here in pulling the rug out from under the concept of man as sub-ject because there is no standing-under (substance) involved. The idea of temporality is eminently qualified to show the inadequacy of the subject to explain experience. We are not describing a subject which somehow "has" experiences; but, rather, the coming about of reality itself.

It is unfortunate that the term "attitude" has been irrevocably relegated to the dustbins of psychology. Attitude is etymologically related to apt and aptitude, fitted or suited for something. An apt remark is a remark which "gets at," suitably characterizes, the situation. An aptitude is an ability, a being *able*, to do something. To be able is, in turn, related to words such as habilitate, to render someone suitable to a new situation which he can then inhabit (dwell in). Thus, one could say that the non-psychological meaning of attitude is the being able to dwell suitably.[10] Attitude is what gives us appropriate, our own, proper, suitable access to what is real. We shall come back to this term "attitude," related to need and attunement, in Chapter Five on the Buddhist Way, to which we now turn. To conclude this Chapter, we might cite an ancient thinker, Heraclitus.

Harmonia aphanes phaneres kreitton.

The harmony (attunement) which does not appear presences more strongly than that which does appear.[11]

CHAPTER 5

The Buddhist Way

The purpose of this chapter is not an explication of Buddhism as such, but rather to see how certain strains of Buddhism deal with the problems we have been discussing in this study: what is reality and what is the nature of our access to reality? The reason for bringing Buddhism into this study at all is not to forage about in rare and exotic doctrines, but rather to see whether Buddhism offers any insights into reality which were not fully developed in the West. Thus, by way of concluding this study, we are not suddenly shifting to some new set of problems, but tentatively inquiring into a different perspective on the same problems we have been discussing.

What does Buddhism have to say about our two fundamental questions regarding the nature of what is real and man's access to that reality? In attempting to answer these questions, the following order might be expedient and fruitful, constantly comparing the results with what has been discovered in the course of this study:

The method—what does Buddhism take as its primary access to what it questions?

The reality—what is the nature of the reality that Buddhism seeks? This question will lead us to the absolutely central and highly complex question of "causality," a causality quite different from that involved in the "reason why."

The Buddhist question about the nature of reality does

not aim at finding out *what* it is, but rather *how it comes about*. Here there is a certain affinity to the problem discussed in Chapter IV of the temporalization of consciousness. But, as we shall see, the Buddhist conception of "time" is radically different from that of Heidegger.

In regard to the term "method," it means literally "way" (*methodos*), and the Buddhist understands it in the profoundly existential sense of a path, a path to be traversed, leading not just to a *knowledge* of reality, but ultimately to *becoming* that reality itself, to discovering one's fundamental identity with it. This is the "mystical" strain so predominant in Eastern thought in general, not only in Buddhism. But the "mysticism" in Buddhism, although not exactly alien to other strains of mysticism, is still quite different from that of Neo-Platonism, Christianity, or even Brahmanism, since Buddhism is unable and unwilling to speak of any kind of "union" of the soul with God. Buddhism accepts neither a soul nor God, and yet it can speak in some sense of "becoming the reality." Thus, we are left with the Western question: "What becomes one with what?", a question that must run into a dead end and finally surrender itself as incommensurate in favor of some other question.

Thus, the method of Buddhism is to be understood quite literally as a path to *reach*, to *attain* something, and not just to acquire theoretical knowledge of it. Buddhist texts are replete with images of the way, focusing on the middle way or path (madhyama-pratipad.) A favorite image is the raft used to cross the stream of birth and death (*samsāra*), then to be discarded, and, generally speaking, the *vehicle* (yāna), used to designate the two central movements of early and later Buddhism, Hīnayāna (Theravāda) and Mahāyāna. The method is not a theoretical means to knowledge, but an existential path to reach "reality."

In addition to being existential, the method or way of Buddhism can further be characterized as pragmatic and as phenomenological, quite in consonance with our modern, Western understanding of these terms. The pragmatism of Buddhism is clear and consistent throughout its many diverse developments, and can be summed up in William James' dictum: "what works is true." The paradigm of pragmatic thinking is perhaps best found in the attitude of the medical doctor. The primary aim of the practicing doctor is not to collect theoretical knowledge about the constitution and elements of various medicines, but to cure his patient. No medicine works the same on every patient, and thus, a knowledge of the effect of a medicine apart from the patient to whom it is given is virtually impossible. Perhaps the most striking example of this pragmatic attitude is the comparison between the seeker after a religion who insists upon having all his questions answered (e.g., does the world have a beginning or not) before he will consent to espouse the religion, with the man wounded by a poison arrow who insists on finding out all about the arrow, what kind of man shot it, what kind of bow, what kind of arrow, etc., before he will allow the surgeon to remove it.[1] In this precarious situation, the questions are obviously irrelevant. The thing to do is remove the poison arrow. If the man persists in his questions, he will die. We might say that if the term "existential" is added to the pragmatic attitude, we have the quality of intense immediacy characteristic of the Buddhist quest.

The question of the phenomenological character of the Buddhist method is a more technical one. For our purposes, it will be sufficient to mention what problems it obviates without delving further into the intricate analyses dedicated to it in the texts. The chief merit of the phenomenological method, developed in the spirit of Kant, is that it presents the world *as experienced by the subject*. A "naive realism" is hardly viable or possible after Kant, who showed that "the conditions *a priori* of any possible experience in general are at the same time conditions of the possibility of any objects of our experience."[2] In other words, experience is the experience of *someone*, the knowing subject is in there and involved, and inseparable from what is being experienced. There is no possible knowledge of, for example, the tree as it is when no one knows it (the tree-or thing-in-itself). The tree is knowable only as phenomenon, as it appears *to* someone.

For the Buddhist, this means that there is no clear-cut dualism between subject and object, between body and mind. Of the dualisms that have plagued Western philosophy, Buddhism does to an extent have to grapple with those of knowing and Being, and of realism and idealism. But the subject-object and the mind-body split are never central; in most cases, they do not even exist.

To return to the question of access and reality, it will ultimately prove untenable to separate these two factors completely. Whereas in most Western philosophy, for example, in Descartes, the point of departure and the method to reach the nature of reality are clearly defined, i.e., to start with the *res cogitans*, (thinking thing) prove the existence of God, and finally regain some certainty about the outside world. Given his philosophical enterprise of finding a *fundamentum inconcussum* (unshakeable foundation) for knowledge, Descartes could not have proceeded any other way than he did. His method is discursive, step by step, and analytical. In Buddhism, when there is a fundamental concept, for example, suffering or pain (*duḥkha*), all the essential concepts relative to it manifest all at once. And if there is real understanding of the "access" to reality, the reality itself is present.

Having stated these difficulties at the outset, let us attempt to see where Buddhism "starts." Descartes started with methodological doubt, and arrived at himself, at the thinking thing. Buddhism starts with the Four Noble Truths, which involve neither a self nor thinking, nor a thing. In the statement that life is suffering, the first of the Four Noble Truths, we already have the other two fundamental statements running through any form of Buddhism, be it Indian, Chinese or Japanese, that all is impermanent and that there is no self. The *fundamentum inconcussum* of Buddhism is unshakable, but, so to speak, unshakable the way an abyss is unshakable. You cannot "shake" what you cannot take hold of. The "foundation" here is bottomless. The only thing "foundational" about it is its absolute *givenness*. It is, so to speak, a foundation which *envelops* us, not something on which we can reach the stability of a "stand." Hopefully, this will become clearer in the following discussion.

The Four Noble Truths, familiar to anyone with an interest in Buddhism, are:

1. And this is the Noble Truth of sorrow. Birth is sorrow, age is sorrow, disease is sorrow; contact with the unpleasant is sorrow, separation from the pleasant is sorrow, every wish unfulfilled is sorrow—in short all the five components of individuality are sorrow.

2. And this is the Noble Truth of the Arising of Sorrow. It arises from craving, which leads to rebirth, which brings delight and passion, and seeks pleasure now here, now there—the craving for sensual pleasure, the craving for continued life, the craving for power.

3. And this is the Noble Truth of the Stopping of Sorrow. It is the complete stopping of that craving, so that no passion remains, leaving it, being emancipated from it, being released from it, giving no place to it.

4. And this is the Noble Truth of the Way which leads to the Stopping of Sorrow. It is the Noble Eightfold Path—Right Views, Right Resolve, Right Speech, Right Conduct, Right Livelihood, Right Effort, Right Mindfulness, and Right Concentration.[3]

The key word for now in the first noble truth is the word *duḥkha* (suffering). Impermanence is probably something more familiar and acceptable to us, although perhaps not to the radical extent that Buddhism proclaims it, than is the fact of *duḥkha*. Everyone has some experience of impermanence: growing older, losing a friend; in a more volatile sense, losing a good mood, a feeling of well-being. And this impermanence does involve pain. But to say that *everything* is impermanent and, beyond that, that *everything* is *pain* would, to the average Westerner, smack of pessimism, not to say nihilism. But the question as to the "meaning of life," if such a question is permitted, does not lie in the facile fabrications of optimism or pessimism. At best, as Nietzsche so powerfully saw, it lies in the question of *affirmation*, of affirmation of life, and that means affirming not just the pleasant and appealing aspects of life, but *all* of life. More importantly and fundamentally, as well shall see, it amounts to a rash snap-judgment which is really no judgment at all, to stamp this statement about impermanence and pain with the imperious seal of the "negative."

We shall take up the question of the Buddhist radicalization of impermanence later, a radicalization that goes beyond any possible empirical "experience" in the normal sense of that term. For now, let us try to understand the statement that life is suffering. We shall start by turning to the tool of etymology which is sometimes helpful and suggestive, sometimes not. We are searching for broader and more "neutral" meanings of *duḥkha* than are implied by the term pain or suffering.

Before going into etymology, let us cite two of many scattered statements to be found in Heidegger on the nature of pain. These statements are always precisely that—statements, suggestive, cryptic and left undeveloped.

> The mystery of pain remains veiled.[4]

> Hence the difference itself remains veiled. A sign of this is the metaphysico-technological reaction to pain which at the same time predetermines the interpretation of the essence of pain[5]

What is suggested in these brief statements is that we (the West) have no access to the true nature of pain; we do everything in our power *not* to experience it, especially in our ever-"developing" technological society whose avoidance of pain borders on the virtuostic.

The Sanskrit etymology of *duḥkha* undeniably embodies a "negative" element, reflected in the prefix "*du*," the opposite of "*su*," (equivalent to the Greek "*eu*," as in euphoria, euthanasia). The root meanings for "*du*" are: uneasy, uncomfortable, unpleasant, difficult.[6] This should remind us of Leibniz' analysis of uneasiness (Locke) and inquietude.[7]

What is philosophically interesting about "suffering" or *duḥkha* is its temporal structure, and this is perhaps what distinguishes it from the undifferentiated, less philosophical, blanket statement that life is simply pain. If Buddhism is not just making a "value judgment" about life in the sense of condemning it as "bad," sorrowful, etc., there must be a more basic and more *neutral* meaning.

The alternative to the statement that life is suffering is not to say that life is joy. We want to undercut this attitude of making either negative or positive value judgments on the worth of life, although existentially speaking, such judgments are not only valid, but almost inevitable. It is very probable that, as long as we are caught up in affective reactions of pronouncing judgment on life situations, we shall never be able to *understand* those situations.

We are attempting to ask about the connection between suffering and impermanence with the aim of getting at the philosophical meaning of the latter in Buddhism.

One of the meanings of suffering is quite simply to undergo or to permit something, as in Christ's statement, "Suffer the little children to come unto me." In this sense, all of our experience is an undergoing of something or, to an increasing degree in the "modern" world, a refusal to undergo certain things by means of a revolt of the *will*. This undergoing, or unwillingness to undergo, seems to be what is meant by the phrase, "*sentient* beings," the beings whom the Buddha as voiced in Mahāyāna Buddhism vowed to save. To be a sentient being means to be able to undergo, feel, experience (go through) things.

One of the most obvious interpretations of being sentient, for which there is also ample basis in earlier Buddhist texts, is to say that all experience is connected with pleasure and pain, and since no pleasure is truly lasting, it is bound to turn into pain when we lose it. This is also copiously documented, for instance, in Schopenhauer, who states that we constantly vacillate between the two poles of pain and *ennui*, or boredom. For Schopenhauer, the nature of life is willing. All willing stems from need and want and lack, and is eventually doomed to land in boredom when it attains what it thought it wanted. But, apart from the obvious kinship of Schopenhauer to Buddhism, Buddhism does not say that all life is a form of some universal will. To be sure, life *begins* with thirst or craving, which in its turn stems from ignorance (*avidyā*). But this ignorance *belongs to no one at all* (no-self), let alone to a universal will.

Since to delve too deeply into Buddhism would be confusing for the purposes of this study, we shall limit ourselves in what follows to the relation of *duḥkha* and impermanence with the aim of understanding the *structure* of impermanence which is instantaneity (*kṣaṇika*). In other words, we want to get at the structure of Buddhist *reality* which is certainly not comprehensible in terms of the reason why, and is ultimately not even so much a matter of "causal conditions," although they are undeniably a major factor in Buddhist analysis. Our two initial, fundamental questions: what is real, and what is man, are now both going to lead us to a dimension of "reality" which is diametrically opposed to the Western conception of reality as what persists through change or does not change at all (substance) and which inextricably involves the "nature" of man in a totally *non-subjective* way. If man is not conceived as a subject, his involvement with reality is not going to be "subjective" or even "psychological."

It seems that two of the issues central to this study come together at this point: the level of experience described as non-rational and the structure of experience described as temporal. We must of necessity proceed very tentatively here in order to avoid conflating things at the expense of losing sight of their differentiation. The pitfall of finally saying that everything is the same yawns before us. We did state that in Buddhism the central ideas are inseparably connected. But they are not "the same."

We are now asking about the relation of the non-rational faculties or *abilities* to experience or undergo something, and "time," the temporality of our awareness. And we shall attempt to link these two factors that have emerged in the course of our study with the two factors in Buddhism now in question: with *duḥkha* and *kṣaṇika*, instantaneity. This could be termed what in German is a *Gedankenexperiment*, an experiment in thinking.

If Heidegger were talking about the relation of the non-rational faculties to time, which in a way he is in part doing, he would define that relation by saying that time or temporality makes the non-rational faculties (*and* the "rational" ones, in his case primarily the existential of understanding) *possible*. Heidegger radicalizes and develops further the Kantian question of the condition of the possibility of experience. Instead of stopping with an unclarified relation between time, as the form of all inner and outer experience, to the "I think," Heidegger lets these two coalesce. Kant was able to say only that the "I think" must be able to accompany all experience, but he never specified the nature of this "accompanying," which is, after all, a rather loose and external relation. If I accompany someone to the supermarket, I just "go along with" him. Heidegger, however, grounds the reality of the self in time or temporality. Temporality makes the full concretion of the phenomenon of *Da-sein* (self) possible.

Is the relation of *duḥkha* and impermanence and ultimately the instantaneity of time a relation of this nature? No. If we can explain why the Buddhist relation is different, we can perhaps use our own kind of *via negativa* to point toward the distinctive nature of the Buddhist conception of reality. That will be, at best, the extent of what can be accomplished in this study.[8]

I am making the attempt—surely controversial, perhaps untenable—to interpret *duḥkha* as a kind of sheer *givenness*. This should not be construed as some kind of naive realism or empiricism. Even when the Buddhists say that life is a dream, we are still talking about a *dream*, about something and not about nothing at all. Something is given in the dream. Something is given, to which we then cling, which we thirst after and try to grasp and hold onto. *But the clinging is not the givenness*, no matter how "universal" this clinging may be. And it is universal. But that does not necessarily mean that clinging is produced by universal, subjectively necessary conditions of the possibility of experience. First of all, the Buddhist is not asking about conditions of possibility as such. What is common to Kant and to Buddhism is that both are saying that this is how experience is. But Kant is saying that *cognitive* experience can *only* be this way.[9] Buddhism is saying that experience has *always been* this way unless something is done about it, unless a radical, non-"natural" and non-automatic change is effected in the way we experience.

Thus, the Buddhist conception of the relation of *duḥkha* and time is not one of conditions of possibility. Time does not make *duḥkha* possible.

Let us now attempt to get a viable English expression for *duḥkha* for our purposes. *Duḥkha* has primarily to do with the *capability* to *feel* (pleasure or pain or indifference, in early Buddhism reduced to the feeling of pain or suffering). *Duḥkha* is *affectability*, the ability to be affected, which we can link to the neutral meaning of "suffering" mentioned before. As bare givenness, before all thirst, clinging and grasping arising from ignorance, *duḥkha* is affectability. Buddhism does not seem to wish to *explain* the givenness of affectability; it is something behind which there is nothing giving or structuring or producing, a givenness with no "giver." Thus, time (or ultimately instantaneity) does not make affectability possible.

But neither is the time of Buddhism the objective framework of Newtonian physics, the objectively present, independent *container* in which things occur unaffected by that time. The time of Buddhism is neither objective nor subjective. It is closer to what we call "subjective," except that Buddhism does not have the subject and is utterly lacking the subject-object split. The time of Buddhism has to do with man in his Buddha-nature, but Buddha-nature is not confined to man. In terms of our question of reality and access to that reality, we could say preliminarily that time is the reality *and* the access to that reality. In the words of Dōgen,[10] being is time. But this is still too "abstract" to be of much help, although Dōgen, coming much later in the Mahāyāna tradition, captured the true spirit of being as related to the notion of time.

The historical background for Dōgen's unique experiential understanding of *uji*, being-time, presumably lies in the general Buddhist tenet that everything is impermanent and in its subsequent radicalization into the doctrine that everything is instantaneous. Whereas the statement that everything is impermanent seems fairly plausible to most people, the statement that everything is instantaneous seems to lack any palpable basis in ordinary experience. I should like to try to examine what happens to the doctrine of instantaneity in Dōgen's thought and to inquire into the implications of that transformation for—what I shall call for lack of a better term—the occurrence of world.

Time. At this point, we need to delve further into the relation of impermanence and instantaneity. As stated before, impermanence is a concept familiar to everyone, but it is not very "precise." My health is impermanent, but *when* does it happen that I lose it? A friendship is impermanent, but *when* does it start to go wrong? Or, to take a broader tack, when does *anything* actually change? How is it that I suddenly get a new idea or even make up my mind to do something? "When"? The general concept of impermanence does not answer any of these questions, and maybe they do not admit of too precise and meaningful an answer in conceptual terms at all. But one should try. If one takes a hard look at it, transience turns out to be incomprehensible, a fact which is forcefully brought home by the death of someone.

The doctrine of instantaneity (*kṣaṇikatvavāda*) radicalizes the early Buddhist truth of impermanence into a unique theory of moments or instants. Reality is instantaneous, i.e., it *occurs* in an instantaneous way. It is not just the case that things gradually "somehow" age and pass away; things are, according to this doctrine, coming into being and passing away constantly *every instant*. Reality is radically discontinuous and discrete. Reality is not the *process* of impermanence. Reality is not a process at all, at which point any similarity between Buddhism and "process philosophy," including Heidegger, stops. Buddhism might say that process is the *degeneration* of the discontinuity of instantaneity into continuity.

It is not necessary for our purposes, nor is it possible in general, considering the stage of advance in available research completed, to trace completely the development of impermanence to instantaneity. We know of interim stages of analyzing the moment into its constitutive factors of arising, persisting and passing away before arriving at the theory that sixty-five instants have come into being and passed away during the time it takes a vigorous young man to snap his fingers. Here we have an absolute lack of duration.

However, we are not primarily concerned with the *measurement* of time here, but with "time" itself; and that means, in Buddhism, instantaneity. If the *meaning* of the doctrine of instantaneity does not lie in measuring the brevity of those instants, we must look for possible dimensions of meaning other than measurement.

We are perhaps now in a position to outline the following points to be discussed in the remainder of this chapter:

"proofs" of instantaneity

Dōgen on *uji* (being-time)

consequences of the nature of time for the nature of
reality

proofs of instantaneity

The doctrine of instantaneity or momentariness is generally
not held to be one of the tenets of Urbuddhism, but to have
become prominent around the time of Buddhaghosa (Fourth to
Fifth centuries A.D.).[1] In the Indian tradition, we find a good
deal of substantial discussion of instantaneity in the *Abhidhar-
makosa* of Vasubandhu and again in Dharmakīrti's *Hetabindu*,
largely in the form of proofs. The *context* for this discussion is
that of the question how something can produce an effect, or,
more broadly in our own formulation, how anything can occur
at all.

These proofs have three points of departure which are not
entirely separable from each other: (1) The principle of contradiction, (2) Existence, and (3) Destruction. We shall try to give
a succinct formulation of all three together in order to provide
a background for understanding *uji* (being-time).

To "exist" means to produce an effect, to be efficacious.[12]
Existence and duration absolutely exclude each other. In duration, conceived as static persistence, nothing can "happen."

If, following the Buddhist tenet, everything is perishable
and impermanent by nature, i.e., if perishing *is* the nature of
things and not just some incidental attribute, everything must
perish as soon as it arises, independently of any external cause
of destruction. If things were not perishable by their very nature,
nothing could destroy them. And yet, we know that they perish.
Thus, everything arises and perishes again and again in every
instant. Reality is instantaneous. If something is to produce an
effect (for the Buddhist, if something is to *exist*), if anything is
to occur, it must occur in the instant. Outside of the instant,
nothing can come about.

To the obvious objection that things perish gradually or
that there are external causes of destruction, for instance, smash-
ing a vase with a hammer, the Buddhist will answer that we
simply fail to notice that things arise and perish in every instant.
In the case of the hammer and vase, the destruction has merely

become empirically evident in a certain action. In reality, the vase comes into existence and perishes constantly.

We are not concerned here with the formal structure of these proofs or even with the question of why these proofs are being given, but rather with the implications of this theory of "time." They are:

1. There is absolutely no duration or even continuity in this time.

2. There is no possible separation between "time" and the things in it.

In the later formulation of Dōgen, existence and time are "identical."

These two statements are interconnected and are capable of further precision. In fact, they are still in a preliminary stage of formulation at this point.

1. Instantaneity and duration absolutely exclude each other. The proofs in terms of destruction attempt to show that, if things are to perish, as they do and must, they must perish of themselves, not from an external cause, but instantly, right away. This means that what we call a thing in the broadest sense of that term is in reality not something substantial or extended with a (limited) duration, not even a thing conceived as being involved in a process, but a disparate succession of "flashings up"[13] (*Auf-blitzen*) of something for which there seems to be no adequate name. It just *is*, i.e., "occurs." The question of "when" something actually changes or comes about turns out to be a spurious and inappropriate one. Something actually changes or occurs "all the time"; in fact, time is nothing but this changing and coming about at every instant in a way hardly accessible to our conceptual thinking that is geared to persisting, relatively stable entities. We think, for example, of the human body as a relatively stable "thing," something that does grow up and grow older "with time." But anyone who introspects a little can realize, if not perceive, that even this relatively stable body whose functioning we generally take for granted is constantly "doing something": breathing, heartbeat and other ac-

tivities which we cannot observe at all, such as cell production. How much more is this true of our minds which are hardly thinking *things*, but a kind of succession of incredibly brief and rapid ideas, impressions, feelings, etc., often quite disorganized. Again, what is important is not the speed (a question of measurement) of this succession, but its character of arising and disappearing, its disparateness, its "verticality."

2. There is no "place" or "room" for an enduring "thing" to be *in* this kind of time. The thing *is* its own occurrence. Our habitual way of thinking and experiencing prevents us from realizing this, but even contemporary physics has come up with a world view not far from it. What I perceive as the desk on which I am writing is in the view of the physicist largely "nothing" interspersed with atoms or whatever the smallest particles are being called this week, whirling around at unbelievable speeds.

Now, what does Dōgen do with the nature of time (*uji*)? His discussion of time is not at all restricted to the chapter bearing that name, but permeates the whole of the *Shōbōgenzō*.

Dōgen retains the two points made above with a slightly different slant which we could formulate as follows:

Nothing changes into anything else, everything is independent and self-contained.

There is an inscrutable identity; each instant, as it is, contains all time and the whole universe in a dynamic sense.

These statements are, of course, a real slap in the face to common sense.

Let us concentrate on the first point. "Time" for Dōgen has nothing to do with duration, and thus has little to do with what we usually think of as time. We think of time in terms of the past, the present and the future, in terms of shorter or longer stretches of time, in terms of "clock time." All of this has its justification and its place in ordinary experience, but it is not what Dōgen is talking about.

Not only does Dōgen deny duration, an idea which is quite contrary to common sense experience. He goes beyond this to deny any kind of *transition* whatsoever. Again, Dōgen is delving into the ultimate nature of time, and not describing our everyday experience of it which is some kind of distortion of ultimate time, no matter how universally prevalent that distortion may be. Viewed from Dōgen's ultimate standpoint, every thing dwells in its dharma situation and exerts itself totally. Dwelling in a dharma situation means, roughly speaking, that every thing has a kind of "world point" in the scheme of things, a position which it does not abandon. A thing does not "pass over" or transit to the next moment, but "dwells" or "stays" where it is. But this dwelling of each thing is not static, it is rather ecstatic,[14] open to a vertical dimension of ultimate reality. "Vertical" is, of course, a makeshift term here, but even Dōgen uses it. In contrast to the *nunc stans*, the standing now of the Western tradition, the moment or instant is not an isolated moment "temporarily" lifted out of time and above time into some kind of eternity. The instant occurs again and again while dwelling in its dharma situation.

Since time and the things in time cannot be separated, we could also say that all things occur again and again in their dharma situations. Nor is Dōgen's analysis of abiding in a dharma situation and exerting oneself totally limited to "consciousness," for example, to the exertion involved in practice. Dōgen has left the subjective idealism of the Mahāyānist consciousness-only school (*vijñānavāda*) behind. The mountain exerts itself totally as well. Thus, the meaning of "exertion," which is obvious in human endeavors, must be broadened to mean something like "totally and dynamically being what it is to the utmost," in order to encompass the mountain. In Dōgen's words, the mountain or a simple human activity enacts "the whole being of emptiness leaping out of itself."[15]

What are the implications of this strange and bold theory of time? With regard to the Buddha nature, Dōgen's name for ultimate reality, it cannot be thought of as something potentially inherent in us which we could develop. There is no development and no transition from potentiality to actuality in this kind of time since the basis for such a continuity is utterly lacking. Thus, the two most prevalent ways of explaining the occurrence of the world, teleology and mechanism, are incompatible with Dōgen's conception of time. Both require a "horizontal" continuity. Mechanism requires a continuum in which some kind of force or energy is transmitted. In the case of teleology, it is even more obvious that the ripening of potentiality into actuality can take place only in some kind of "bearer" or continuous substratum of that process.

With regard to our question of the nature of reality, for Dōgen, to explain what is real by giving the reason why for it makes little or no sense. Every thing has a before and an after—that defines its dharma situation—but the before and after are together in the moment, not outside of it. They constitute, so to speak, the dimensionality of the moment. Thus, in an inquiry into the nature of what is real, the question of *why* something is misses the point. The thing just *is*. Here we may note a strong affinity to Spinoza for whom everything is necessary, but not necessary from any external constraint, and to Eckhart's statements about the is-ness (*Istigkeit*) of things. There is also a marked affinity between Eckhart's releasement (*Gelassenheit*) and Dōgen's more concrete expression, "dropping off body and mind." Such "affinities" can at best help to give some orientation on the connection of Dōgen with Western thinking. However difficult Dōgen may be, and he *is* difficult, he is a *thinker*, and as such must be at least partially accessible and intelligible to anyone who makes the effort to understand him and shares some of his experience.

It is difficult at this point to assess exhaustively the philosophical import of being-time. Being-time harbors no elaborate structures in itself; it is not a kind of creative evolution (Bergson), nor has it the *constitutive* temporal structures that we find in Heidegger. It is, so to speak, sheer, dynamic, discrete occurrence of every instant. This means that the instants are not "produced" by the preceding instant, and, in their turn, do not produce a succeeding instant. The instants are *self-generating*.

Let us try at least to reflect upon some of the statements of this extremely bold, original and difficult thinker.

> Abandon notions of outside and inside, coming and going. Undivided mind is not outside or inside: it comes and goes freely without attachment. One thought: mountain, water, earth. Next thought, a new mountain, water, earth. Every thought is independent, newly created, vital, instantaneous.

... We should accept things as they come—i.e., independent and momentary....

When a monk was asked the question, what is the original Buddha-mind, he replied, "Wall, fence, tiles, stones...." "Wall, fence, tiles, stones" symbolize "everyday mind." This mind is not concerned with the past or future worlds—it is continually working now, in the present, and concerns itself only with *each new moment*. "Everyday mind" is its own accomplishment, self-contained and self-fulfilling. Ancient times are cut off and past, present and future exist together in each moment.

"... 'Everyday mind' opens its gates for each moment of existence—life and death, coming and going enter freely. Do not think of heaven and earth as this world or the next; know that they co-exist eternally in each passing moment. Generally, people never think about the nature of heaven and earth unless something unexpected occurs. For me, a sudden and unexpected sneeze is like an echo that symbolizes the instantaneous coexistence of life and death, heaven and earth in each moment. The entire content and meaning of heaven and earth and its relationship to the mind reduces itself to one eternal moment. If we fail to understand this we will never grasp the significance of a sneeze or any seemingly minor occurrence.[16]

Every thought is independent, newly created, vital, instantaneous. It is no wonder that Dōgen made "time" absolutely central in his thinking. If one understands what he means by being-time, that is, an incredibly "rapid" succession of discrete, "dynamic" instants, many of the basic tenets of Buddhism become *concretely* intelligible. If "time" affords no substratum or duration at all, there can be no ego persisting in that time. One could say that our ordinary conception of the ego is based upon a false view of time, a view that *we generate*. We fail to experience the enormous dynamic of instantaneity, delude ourselves that "time goes on and on," and cling to the notion of our own duration and persistence. The notion of an ego is generally held to be based on the memory of the past and on the possible anticipation of the future. If one is able to experience what

Dōgen means by time, there is simply no "room" for a persisting ego. This does not, of course, exclude the fact that we can and must function in terms of a certain "durational," everyday clock time. Dōgen does not deny common sense experience. Rather, he consistently tries to look at precisely that everyday experience in a *totally new way.* Thus, he takes many statements from Buddhist scriptures and turns them around, so to speak, so that they suddenly yield a completely new meaning. It is as if things had somehow become "upside down," and Dōgen uses the method of paradox to put them back on their feet again. "The mountain flows, the river sits."

If one moment does not produce the next, it is no longer tenable to speak of the reason why of something, nor of thinking or doing something for the sake of something else. "Causality" in the usual meaning of that term, whether it is a matter of the reason why or of purposiveness, is incompatible with the occurrence of existence or being. This is not, however, an impoverishment of reality, however negative it may sound. On the contrary, instead of projecting our experience back to the past in searching for a reason why, instead of projecting our experience into the future in the form of purposes, doing things for the sake of something (else), everything is concentrated and condensed into the present, a present which is not static, but occurs constantly. This, and nothing else, is Dōgen's eternal now. Unlike the *nunc stans* of the Western medieval tradition, this eternal present is not lifted out of time. There is, so to speak, no time from which it could be lifted out. Each instant, as it is, is an (the) eternal present. Our problem seems to be that it is extraordinarily difficult to experience this "as it is," or suchness, of the instant. Our discursive thinking spins out, and then divides up, time. Roughly speaking, we "horizontalize" the vertical instants into a prolonged duration to which we then cling.

In attempting to discuss Dōgen, we are no longer capable of following a sequential train of thought, but are somehow forced to keep circling around the seminal issues. Evidently, this must be required by the "matter itself."

Another astounding consequence of Dōgen's understanding of time is that time is not necessarily *irreversible.* If continuity and transition are lacking between the instants, time is not essentially irreversible. It is not so much the case that time can actually be reversed, as that it is never essentially irreversible in the first place. *We* project ourselves "horizontally" into the future, or compare our present state with a past that is "lost forever," and thus create the irreversibility of time. Given Dōgen's analysis of vertically occurring, discrete instants, there is no reason whatsoever why time must be irreversible. This does not, of course, mean that we can literally, physically, "go backwards" in time and become infants again. And who would wish to do that? The body is the bearer of karma in a way that is more inevitable and final (i.e., physical death) than in the case of the "mind." The body can be construed as the result of past karma which totally lacks any arbitrariness. The future is open, and grants the dimension of freedom.

But now we can no longer repress the obvious question: Why is this experience of time that Dōgen is talking about so *rare*? The Brahmanist or Hinduist could answer simply *māyā*, the veil of illusion. The Buddhist can answer *avidyā*, ignorance. We could perhaps venture to say that for Dōgen, ignorance is not a *state* in which we are, but is something we constantly produce *in every moment* due to the attachment to objects in the "horizontal" flow of time.

Dōgen is aware of this problem.

> We realize that each and every aspect of existence is detached and forms an unique independent existence, i.e., Buddha-nature. This is called 'Body and mind drop off.' This realization is dynamic, nothing like the static existence of a Buddha statue. However, do not expect this truth to appear easily without effort; without effort the truth remains hidden. 'Body and mind drop off' represents universal truth, real existence in the present, that neither reverts to the past, nor jumps ahead to the future."[17]

This is strangely reminiscent of Heraclitus' "Nature loves to hide." Reality is "hidden," it keeps to itself. An enormous effort is required to reach it; in fact, this "effort" somehow *belongs* to reality and is integral to its manifestation. Again, effort and sustained exertion, of which Dōgen speaks so often, are most obvious in the case of human beings, but there is still no element of subjectivity involved here. For Dōgen, the mountain exerts itself, too. To speak in Heidegger's terminology, the mountain *presences*; it is not just somehow there as an objectively present, static object.

For Dōgen, mountains and rivers manifest and actualize the Buddha-nature. Here at last is a thinker for whom "nature" is central, not subordinated to "spirit" and inferior to it because it lacks so-called "mind."

> The present mountains and rivers actualize the Way of the ancient Buddhas. Both mountains and rivers maintain their true form and actualize their real virtue. They transcend time and therefore are active in the eternal present.
>
> The priest Fuyo Dokai of Mt. Taiyo said to an assembly: "The green mountains are always moving and a stone woman gives birth at night."
>
> The mountain possesses complete virtue with nothing lacking; therefore, it is always safely rooted, yet constantly moving. We must study the virtue of this "movement" in detail. Simply because the movement of a mountain is not like the movement of a human being, do not doubt that it exists. Dokai's "moving" contains the essence of moving. We must clarify the meaning of 'always moving.' 'Always moving' means eternal. The movement of 'always' is faster than the wind, but those living on the mountain neither realize nor know it. Living on the mountain is analogous to 'When a flower blooms, spring exists everywhere.' However, those who are not on the mountain are also unaware of its movement. Anyone who does not see the mountain for himself cannot realize, see, or hear it due to this principle. If anyone doubts the movement of the mountain, it is because he does not understand his own movement. People move and take steps, but they are unable to understand it. When we understand our own movement, we can understand the movement of the mountain."[18]

Dogen's philosophical task is unique. His use of language attempts to avoid a fundamental dualism that has been given little explicit attention: the dualism of *literal-mindedness* and *philosophical abstraction*. This amounts to the old question of the literal and the symbolic, and Dōgen steers a precarious passage unerringly between the two. That accounts for much of the strangeness and newness of his thinking.

Things are now what they seem, nor are they otherwise.[19]

If things are not what they seem, we cannot start out with a literal-minded point of view, and then buoy ourselves up to something symbolic. The phrase "nor are they otherwise" points to the fact that the "seeming" of things is by no means arbitrary or detachable from "things."

We have already pointed out some of the unique features of Dōgen's conception of being-time: the discreteness of the moments, the fact that each moment contains the whole universe and the fact that there is no possible separation between time and what occurs "in" it, i.e., there is no abstract, separate container-time. Dōgen's time admits of no duration and no transition on the ultimate level. Finally, there is a new principle in Dōgen which extends beyond the realm of time to cover such things as Buddha-nature, functional interdependence, activity, good and evil. We might call this principle the principle of irreversible, transitive identity. This principle is familiar to us in logic, but Dōgen's use of it is completely *ontological*.

Examples:

Good and evil are time, but time is not good and evil. Good and evil are the Dharma, but the Dharma is not good or evil.[20]

'All the Buddhas' are like the gods of total freedom. Even though they have some points in common, the gods of total freedom are not all the Buddhas.[21]

It should be examined and understood thoroughly that functional interdependence (*engi*) is activity, because activity is not functionally interdependent.[22]

If we take these statements logically, they are similar to saying that all dogs are animals, but not all animals are dogs. "Animals" is the broader concept under which "dog" can be subsumed. But since Dōgen is not concerned with logic, or, for that matter, with psychology or anthropology or biology, these statements must be taken in an ontological and a cosmological

sense. We could rephrase the first example to read: good and
evil cannot *be* without time (for Dōgen, nothing can), but time
can *be* without good and evil. Time is not dependent upon good
and evil, the Buddhas are not dependent upon the gods of total
freedom, activity is not dependent upon functional
interdependence.

Dōgen has formulated the law of identity here as a kind of
one-way principle that cannot simply be reversed as in the case
of the basic formulation of the law of identity, A = A. His principle also extends to the relation of man and the Buddha-nature.
If so-called "pantheism"—the term generally betrays a misun-
derstanding of the thinker in question, for instance Spinoza or
Emerson—states that God is "in" the world, Dōgen is stating
that man is in the Buddha-nature. This simply blocks out any
kind of spatial representation of what is being said. It also means
that the Buddha-nature cannot be restricted to man or the world
or anything else. To say that man is the Buddha-nature means
to point to a *way* in which man *is*. It does not describe *where*
he is or even *what* he is, but rather *how* he is. If I say that I am
in a good mood, this has nothing to do with spatial location.

> *Garbha*, in *tathāgata-garbha*, refers either to 'embryo,' which
> is the potentiality to become Tathāgata, or to 'womb,' which
> gives birth to Tathāgata. *Garbha* in the sense of 'store' ... may
> also be interpreted either as the Tathāgata 'hidden' in sentient
> beings or as the Tathāgata which 'embraces' sentient beings.
> In both cases ... the first meaning seems to have been conceived
> at the early stages of *tathāgata-garbha* thought. In one case the
> *tathāgata-garbha* is in *man*, whereas in the other man is in the
> *tathāgata-garbha*. In the former, *tathāgata-garbha* is the po-
> tentiality to become a Buddha which is conceived psychologi-
> cally and anthropologically; in the latter, it is a metaphysical
> or ontological vision of ultimate reality in which men are the
> constituents of the *tathāgata-garbha*.[23]

> The Buddha-nature is all existences which include sentient beings
> and insentient beings, and is no longer the possession of these
> beings. As a result, the absolute inclusiveness of the Buddha-
> nature does not mean that the Buddha-nature is immanent in
> all existences but that all existences are immanent in the Bud-
> dha-nature.[24]

What are the implications of this "principle of irreversible transitive identity" for our study? Simply stated, our basic question is that of the relation of man and reality. Instead of asking why something is (reason why) or for what purpose, the relation to reality indicated here is that of *becoming* (the) reality, or, if that is still too dualistic, of realizing that one already *is* (the) reality. For this, we do not need to "do" anything; rather, we need to *quit* doing whatever it is we are constantly doing, blocking, hindering, obstructing ourselves, mostly unawares.

> Dōgen's concern here is not how and why all existences are as they are, but simply *that* all existences exist in thusness—in this simple *fact* does he find the Buddha-nature.[25]
>
> Not how the world is, is the mystical, but *that* it is.[26]

A "naturalistic" explanation of man is woefully inadequate. Man has not evolved out of some primeval slime (from what did the primeval slime evolve?) to attain the pre-human state of the ape[27] and finally to become the animal with reason. Nor is a teleological explanation more satisfying. Man is not created in order to be the culmination of the world of nature (this has become increasingly difficult to believe). Nevertheless, man did not create himself, his existence is essentially a *gift*. This may be hard to swallow when the "gift" is encumbered with problems, frustrations, worry and suffering, but they *belong* to the gift. What we must do is to stop making value judgments about what we like or do not like, what we want or do not want, and see what is *there*. Without our affectability—which includes suffering—we would never be able to see what is *there*, to see reality.

> Our body is not really ours. Our life is easily changed by time and circumstances and never remains static. Countless things pass and we will never see them again. Our mind is also continually changing. Some people wonder, 'if this is true, on what can we rely?' But others, who have the resolve to seek enlightenment, use this constant flux to deepen their enlightenment.[28]

In conclusion, let us ask about the *meaning* of Dōgen's analysis of being-time. We stated that two outstanding features of being-time were that it admits of no duration or even transition and that each moment, as it is, contains the whole universe. These two features answer the question of why we are to understand that time is not only flying past. In contrast to the ordinary view that everything is in time which is passing by and slipping away, Dōgen says that things *are* precisely the instant present which dwells in its dharma situation by virtue of impeding itself. What is impeding? When something is impeded, it is stopped, stabilized in its own individuality without becoming thus rigidified. When the moon is impeded by water, to use a favorite Buddhist image, it is *reflected* in the water and, so to speak, sees itself. Yet the moon does not obstruct or block or interfere with the water nor does the water interfere with the moon.

Thus, Dōgen can say that spring does not become summer.

> Springtime's passage invariably passes through spring. Passage is not spring (irreversible identity), but since it is the springtime's passage, passing attains the Way now in the time of spring."[29]

We could perhaps say that spring does not pass by and pass away into summer, but that spring comes to pass and takes place, takes its place (dharma-position) as spring. The linguistic difference between passing and coming to pass is rather subtle, but the existential difference constitutes a veritable chasm. As the Zen people say, "a hair's breadth makes all the difference."

As for the feature that each moment, as it is, contains the whole universe, we must now mention something we have neglected up to now: roughly speaking, exertion and activity as manifestation (*ippō-gūjin, gyōji, genjō-kōan*). World cannot become manifest without continuous sustained exertion or activity, but we do not produce or create this activity. It occurs, so to speak, through us. The person sitting on his cushion or arranging flowers is not supposed to be *doing* anything. Rather, he is supposed to *stop* doing whatever it is he is constantly doing, blocking, hindering, obstructing himself without being aware of it. He must allow manifestation to occur through him.

This is not activity in the usual sense of the word, although it may be very strenuous.

Waddell in his translation of the chapter in the *Shōbōgenzō* called "*Uji*" (*Being Time*) describes this activity as follows: "Thus, entirely worlding the entire world with the whole world, is called *penetrating exhaustively*." He adds a footnote: "Time (=being; the creature, the buddha, etc.) realizes or manifests the entire world as itself ("sets itself out in array"). Nothing can be left out of this exhaustive reciprocal penetration (or mutual interpenetration) of all dharmas, in which no room exists for subject/object dichotomy."[30]

"We" world the entire world with the whole world, thus penetrating exhaustively. The repeated emphasis on "whole" or "entire" has to do not with quantity or measurement, but is rather to be understood adverbially as "completely," "entirely," "exhaustively," "utterly." Nothing is left over or left out.

All dharmas in their entirety become exhaustively penetrated by "us" and manifest in us, and this phenomenon Dōgen calls "worlding." Instead of stating that the world is, or what it is, he attempts to say how world worlds, how world comes about, comes to pass. He shows the occurrence of world.

Dōgen's view of time is quite clearly expressed by the late Japanese thinker Hajime Tanabe in an essay entitled "Dialectic of Death (*Todesdialektik*)." Speaking about the concept of Repetition in Kierkegaard, Tanabe states: "The eternal is not 'without beginning and unborn,' but rather comes to an end in each present and at the same time begins anew again and again."[31]

The "positive" aspect of time's coming to pass (*kyōryaku*) as opposed to its negative aspect of passing away is rather neatly expressed by the following brief anecdote with which I close.

A certain Zen master was discussing one of his students whom he had known and seen from time to time over a period of many years. He was commenting on this person's stubbornness, rigidity and inability to change or grow. Finally, he said with a profound sigh: "You know, sometimes impermanence doesn't work!"

There is really no definite conclusion to this study. We are unable to summarize these chapters with some kind of magic formula about the relation of man to reality, a formula which would no longer be "valid" next week, or tomorrow, or in the next moment. *There is* something very real, but real not in the sense of extended things or thinking things (Descartes) or of objective presence (Heidegger's polemic). Man has a privileged access to that reality in that he can become or *be* it (in the transitive sense of be or exist). In Dōgen's words, he can "exert himself" in his own way, just as the mountain "exerts itself" and comes to presence dynamically. And man's ability or potential to exert himself and come to presence and be reality is afforded by his affectability, an affectability which by no means excludes reason. But Western thinkers up to the nineteenth century have predominantly attempted to dominate and control or eliminate this element of affectability which is absolutely crucial to our experience. The attempt in the nineteenth century to exalt the irrational only distorted the element of affectability. There is nothing irrational about being affected. Affectability can be rational or non-rational, or at times, supra-rational.

To conclude what can be said about Buddhism in general at this point, Buddhism offers a possibility of existential experiencing which is neither merely causally determined nor teleological. To live as if our experience of the moment is always determined by the past (as exemplified, for example, *par excellence*, in Freudian psychology) amounts to never being truly able to experience the present as it is. Rationalism and the constant search for reasons why make us attempt to *explain* the present in terms of the past, instead of experiencing the present as present. And to live as if every moment and everything we do is always for the sake of something *else* again amounts to losing the experience of the present. This is not to deny a conventional meaning of past and future, but rather not to allow these conceptual ideas of past and future to overwhelm and choke the experience of the present. Whatever else the philosophical implications of the Buddhist "theory" of instantaneity are, it underscores the radical discreteness of the moment which refuses to be drawn into the continuity of a merely causal or a teleological continuum. It is also this conceptual continuity which blocks the affectability of the moment and the richness and intensity of experience which it affords.

Notes

Chapter 1

1. Immanuel Kant, *Critique of Pure Reason*, trans. by F. Max Müller, New York, Anchor Books, 1966, p. 107, A111.

2. Plato, *Collected Dialogues*, ed. Hamilton and Cairns, New York, Random House, 1963, *Republic*, 510.

3. One of the four moments of the aesthetic judgment of a work of art is that it be "without interest", i.e. without concern for the factual existence of the thing.

4. Op. cit., *Theatetus*, 206d.

5. *The Basic Works of Aristotle*, ed. Richard McKeon, New York, Random House, pp. 67–71, 1941, *Politics* 1332b.

6. See Chapter 2 in this volume.

7. Op. cit., *Politics*, 1340.

8. Ibid. 1334.

9. Op. cit., *Republic*, 617e.

10. Op. cit., *Phaedrus*, 238c.

11. Ibid., 247d.

12. Ibid., 247e.

13. Op. cit., *Republic*, 588e.

14. Ibid., 590.

15. The efficient cause comes to be called cause proper in the later sense of that word.

16. In the mind, contrary to the use of that term with and after Kant, *Formaliter.*

17. *Formaliter* in the old Aristotelian sense of form as actuality.

18. G.W. Leibniz, *Selections*, ed. Philip P. Wiener, New York, Scribners, 1951, "Monadology," sec. 79.

19. Ibid., ¶ 87.

20. Ibid., ¶ 17.

21. Ibid.

22. Ibid.

23. Op. cit., *Discourse on Metaphysics*, XVIII.

24. Op. cit., *The Principles of Nature and Grace Based on Reason*, no. 7.

25. Op. cit., *On The Ultimate Origin of Things*, p. 347.

26. Ibid.

27. Cf. Arthur Lovejoy, *The Great Chain of Being*, New York, Harper Torchbook, 1960 for an excellent discussion of this question.

28. *Die Philosophischen Schriften von G.W. Leibniz*, ed. Gerhardt, Hildesheim, Olms, 1965, vol. 7, Leibniz Fourth Paper; "Being an Answer to Dr. Clarke's Third Reply," ¶ 5, p. 372.

29. Op. cit., Leibniz' Fifth Paper: "Being an Answer to Dr. Clarke's Fourth Reply," ¶ 17, p. 392.

30. Ibid., ¶ 21.

31. Ibid., ¶ 89.

32. Ibid.

33. Immanuel Kant, *Critique of Pure Reason*, Garden City, Doubleday 1966, B25.

34. Immanuel Kant, *Critique of Judgement*, New York, Hafner, 1951, ¶ 84.

35. Op. cit., *Critique of Pure Reason*, B75, A51.

36. Ibid., A156–160, B195–199.

37. Ibid., A166, B207.

38. Ibid., B242, A197.

39. Op. cit., *Critique of Judgement*, Introduction, ¶ IV.

40. Ibid., ¶ 70.

41. Ibid., Introduction IX, note.

42. Cf. *Critique of Pure Reason* A805, B833.

43. Op. cit., *Critique of Judgement*, ¶ 91.

44. Cf. Kant's furious criticism of Swedenburg in *Träume eines Geistersehers, erläutert durch Träume der Metaphysik.*

45. G.F.W. Hegel, *The Phenomenology of Spirit*, Preface, Baillie translation p. 104, and the chapter on "Absolute Knowledge," Baillie translation p. 800, in *Selections*, New York, Scribner, 1929.

46. Ibid.

47. *Encyclopedia*, ¶ 44.

48. *Encyclopedia*, ¶ 50.

49. Ibid., ¶ 60.

50. Preface, *Phenomenology.*

Chapter 2

1. In a larger and different context, *De Anima* also treats the non-rational, i.e. *sub*-rational faculties of the soul, analyzed as its nutritive and sentient aspects.

2. *Rhetoric* I, 10, 1369.

3. Ibid., I, 11, 1370.

4. Ibid., II, 1, 1377.

5. Cf. "Monodology," sec. 17.

6. *Ethics* III, end.

7. Ibid., III, Definition III.

8. Ibid., III, proposition VI. This endeavor to persist in its being is the very essence of the thing.

9. Ibid., II, proposition XL.

10. Ibid., V, proposition XXXVI.

11. Ibid., IV, end.

12. Ibid., IV, appendix, proposition XXXI.

13. Martin Heidegger, *Being and Time*, trans. Macquarrie and Robinson, New York, Harper and Row, 1962.

14. G.W. Leibniz, *New Essays*, Hildesheim, Olms Verlag, 1965, vol. 5, pp. 373–374.

15. Ibid., p. 377.

16. Ibid., XX, ¶ 1.

17. Ibid., XX ¶ 6

18. A comparable instance can be seen in the word innocence (literally what cannot be injured or harmed) which has no negative connotations.

19. Ibid., ¶ 6.

20. Ibid.

21. Ibid., ¶ 8.

Chapter 3

1. Johannes Hoffmeister, *Wörterbuch der philosophischen Begriffe*. Hamburg, Felix Meiner, 1955, pp. 337–8.

2. F. Nietzsche, *The Will to Power*, Tr. by Walter Kaufmann and R. J. Hollingdale, New York, Random House, 1967.

3. For a more detailed discussion of this problem, cf. my *Nietzsche's Thought of Eternal Return*, Baltimore, Johns Hopkins University Press, 1972, pp. 76–82.

4. As we say of an irrational number that it cannot be expressed exactly.

5. Arthur Schopenhauer, *The World as Will and Idea*, New York, Modern Library, 1956, p. 248.

6. Ibid., p. 285.

7. Ibid., p. 335.

8. Kafka's conception of the absurd is on a different level and has a positive relation to meaningfulness.

9. Aristotle in the *Rhetoric* made the observation that the compulsive person is unfree in the highest possible sense. His actions are voluntary, but unfree in that they serve no purpose.

10. Cf. "A Note on the Unconscious in Psychoanalysis," (1912) in *A General Selection from the Works of Sigmund Freud*, New York, Doubleday, 1957.

11. Sigmund Freud, *On Creativity and the Unconscious* (1919), New York, Harper Torchbooks, 1958, pp. 122–61.

12. Cf. Sigmund Freud, "One of the Difficulties of Psycho-Analysis," (1917), Ibid., pp. 1–10.

13. The precarious balance, imbalance and conflict of the ego, superego and id, to take the simplest formulation, leaving out the problems of the reality principle, pleasure principle and death instinct.

14. Cf. "One of the Difficulties of Psycho-Analysis," (1917) in *On Creativity and the Unconscious*, pp. 1–10.

15. Ibid., p. 9.

16. "Monadology", No. 61. For a fuller *historical* treatment, cf. pp. 61–69 of this study.

17. Rollo May, "The Origins and Significance of the Existential Movement in Psychiatry," in *Existence*, New York, Simon & Schuster, 1967, p. 5.

18. D.T. Suzuki, *The Zen Doctrine of No-Mind*, Rider and Company, London, 1958, p. 71.

19. Ibid., pp. 69–70.

20. Ibid., p. 125.

Chapter 4

1. Martin Heidegger, *Being and Time*, New York, Harper and Row, 1962, p. 175.

2. For a delightful satire on the current fashionability of time,

the time fad, cf. Wyndham Lewis, *Time and Western Man* (Boston, Beacon Press, 1957).

3. Op. cit., *Being and Time*, p. 170, translation mine.

4. Cf. my brief introduction to Martin Heidegger, *The End of Philosophy*, New York, Harper and Row, 1973.

5. *Zu-kunft*, literally coming toward.

6. Cf. "What is Metaphysics?" in Martin Heidegger, *Basic Writings*, New York, Harper and Row, 1977.

7. Henri Bergson, *Duration and Simultaneity*, New York: Bobbs-Merrill, 1965, p. 44.

8. *Befindlichkeit*, literally how I find myself. *Wie befinden Sie sich*, how are you, how do you find yourself?

9. Cf. "Building, Dwelling, Thinking," in Martin Heidegger, *Poetry, Language and Thought*, trans. Albert Hofstadter, New York: Harper and Row, 1971, pp. 145–161.

10. Perhaps I may here be permitted a play on words, which is feasible only in German. Something suitable is something like us, which we like. The German for liking is *Moegen*, which would be the possible new dimension for relating to things, as opposed to *Vermoegen*, faculty. This play on words is, at best, suggestive.

11. Standard translation (Diels): "Invisible harmony *(Fügung)* is stronger than visible.

Chapter 5

1. "Questions which tend not to Edification," sermon no. 1, quoted in *World of the Buddha*, New York, Anchor Books, 1969, pp. 143–49.

2. Op. Cit., *Critique of Pure Reason*, A 11.

3. Quoted in de Bary, *The Buddhist Tradition*, N.Y.: Vintage Books, 1969, p. 16–17.

4. "What are Poets for?" in Martin Heidegger, *Poetry, Language and Thought*, trans. Albert Hofstadter, New York, Harper and Row, 1971, p. 96.

5. *The End of Philosophy*, p. 91.

6. *A Sanskrit-English Dictionary*, Sir M. Monier-Williams, Oxford, Clarendon Press, 1960. p. 483.

7. Cf. Chapter Two, pp. 90–94.

8. I hope to pursue this question further in another study focussed on Buddhism alone.

9. Cf. Kant, "Dreams of a spiritual seer," "Träume eines Geistersehers, *Vorkritische Schriften,*" vol. II, de Gruyter, Berlin, 1968.

10. Dōgen Kigen, *Shōbōgenzō*, "Uji," trans. N.A. Waddell in *The Eastern Buddhist*, vol. XII, no. 1, pp. 116–129.

11. Cf. David J. Kalupahana, *Causality. The Central Problem of Buddhism*, Honolulu, University of Hawaii Press, 1976, p. 148 ff.

12. Here we see that "existence" is as far removed as possible from persistence, or what Heidegger calls objective presence (*Vorhandenheit*).

13. Cf. Leibniz who spoke of "fulgurations." "Monadology" sec. 47.

14. Here indeed there is an affinity to Heidegger's analysis of existence as standing out and as standing in (*Inständigkeit*, instant). *Inständigkeit* is perdurance, which may be related to Dōgen's sustained exertion.

15. Quoted in *Dōgen Kigen—Mystical Realist*, Hee-jin Kim, The University of Arizona Press, Tucson, Arizona, 1975, p. 201. This study is extremely helpful and valuable for anyone interested in understanding Dōgen philosophically. Cf. by the same author a later article, "Existence/Time as the Way of Ascesis" in *The Eastern Buddhist*, vol. VI no. 2, pp. 43–73.

16. Dōgen Kigen, *Shōbōgenzō* vol. I, "Shinjingakudō," trans. Kōsen Nishiyama and John Stevens. Sendai: Daihokkaikaku Publishing Co., 1975, pp. 11–13.

17. Op. cit., Shōbōgenzō, vol. I, "Sokushinzebutsu," p. 19.

18. Ibid., *Shōbōgenzō*, vol. II, "Sansuikyō," p. 163.

19. *Laṅkāvatara Sūtra*, as quoted by Eidō Shimano Rōshi.

20. Op. cit., *Shōbōgenzō*, vol. II, "Shoakumakusa," p. 171.

21. Ibid., p. 174.

22. Quoted in Kim, op. cit., p. 94. *Engi* refers to interdependent or interrelational origination (pratītya-samutpāda).

23. Ibid., p. 145.

24. Ibid., p. 164.

25. Ibid., p. 168.

26. Ludwig Wittgenstein, *Tractatus Logico-Philosophicus*, London, Routledge and Kegan Paul, 1958, 6.44.

27. Karl Jaspers, *The Perennial Scope of Philosophy*, New York, Philosophical Library, 1949, p. 59.

28. Op. cit., *Shōbōgenzō*, vol. I, "Immo," p. 58. Cf. also "... without realizing that the dis-ease itself is the root of enlightenment," ibid., *Kūge*, p. 49, hyphen mine.

29. Dōgen, "Being-time," *op. cit.*, p. 124.

30. Ibid., p. 122, fn. 29.

31. *Martin Heidegger zum 70. Geburtstag*, Neske, Pfullingen, 1959, p. 119.

Index

129